Is There a Universal Grammar of Religion?

The Master Hsüan Hua Memorial Lecture series
General Editor: Martin J. Verhoeven

The First Master Hsüan Hua Memorial Lecture
Rationality and Religious Experience: The Continuing Relevance of the World's Spiritual Traditions
Henry Rosemont, Jr.

The Second Master Hsüan Hua Memorial Lecture
Worldly Wonder: Religions Enter Their Ecological Phase
Mary Evelyn Tucker

The Third Master Hsüan Hua Memorial Lecture is not available as a book in this series; published as "On State and Religion in China: A Brief Historical Reflection," *Religion East and West* 3 (June 2003): 1–20.

The Fourth Master Hsüan Hua Memorial Lecture
Our Spiritual Crisis: Recovering Human Wisdom in a Time of Violence
Michael N. Nagler

The Fifth Master Hsüan Hua Memorial Lecture
Is There a Universal Grammar of Religion?
Henry Rosemont, Jr., and Huston Smith

Is There a Universal Grammar of Religion?

HENRY ROSEMONT, JR.
and
HUSTON SMITH

With the assistance of
Martin J. Verhoeven and David Rounds

The Fifth Master Hsüan Hua
Memorial Lecture

OPEN COURT
Chicago and La Salle, Illinois

To order books from Open Court, call toll-free 1-800-815-2280, or
visit our website at www.opencourtbooks.com.

Open Court Publishing Company is a division of Carus Publishing Company.

Library of Congress Cataloging-in-Publication Data

Rosemont, Henry, 1934-
    Is there a universal grammar of religion? / Henry Rosemont, Jr. and Huston
Smith ; with the assistance of Martin J. Verhoeven and David Rounds.
    p. cm. — (The master Hsuan Hua memorial lecture series) (The fifth
master Hsuan Hua memorial lecture)
    Summary: "Huston Smith proposes the idea of a Universal Grammar of
Religion and claims fourteen points of substantial identity among all the
great religious traditions. Includes Henry Rosemont's response and final
reflection, and a conversation between the two"— Provided by publisher.
    Includes bibliographical references and index.
    ISBN 978-0-8126-9644-8 (trade paper : alk. paper)
    1. Religion. I. Smith, Huston. II. Verhoeven, Martin. III. Rounds, David.
IV. Title.
BL48.R547 2008
200—dc22

                                  2008008663

CONTENTS

PREFACE

*I*n 1958, with the publication of *The Religions of Man*, later revised as *The World's Religions*, Huston Smith brought before the American public a new way of thinking about religion. He was not the first Christian scholar to have studied the various scriptures of the great religions and among them to have found deep consonances that far outweigh the differences. What Professor Smith added to this was a courageous open-mindedness that allowed him to go beyond merely literary comparisons and to actively participate in the daily observances and the esoteric practices of other religions. Having grown up in China as the son of missionaries, he traveled to Muslim countries and sat at the feet of Sufi masters; he lived in Japan and joined Zen monks in their practice of still meditation; he studied the Vedanta in India. With these and other such experiences, he was able, in his groundbreaking book, to describe the world's religions with a fresh authority. In simple language that was nevertheless not reductive, he was able to get to the heart of what religions actually mean to the people who practice them. His conclusion was that all religions can serve their adherents in the same ways. Each is based on underlying propositions that reappear in the others. Therefore it is plain, he argued, that all religions have validity and deserve equal respect.

Since the initial publication of *The Religions of Man*, in the books that have followed it and in countless lectures and interviews, Professor Smith has continued to argue for the indispensable value and the fundamental equality of the world's religions. Now well into his ninth decade, Professor Smith offers, in the present small volume, a final distillation of his lifetime of study, practice, and insight. He describes a Universal Grammar of religion, in which he claims fourteen points of substantial identity among all the great traditions. Since these points, he argues, are universals, it is evident that a capacity to respond to them must belong to the innate psychophysical makeup of human beings. Borrowing language from the generative linguist Noam Chomsky, who was his friend and colleague at the Massachusetts Institute of Technology, Professor Smith concludes that we are hard-wired with a capacity for religious experience in the same way that Chomsky claims we are hard-wired to speak our native tongues within the constraints of the syntactic patterns that collectively comprise "Universal Grammar."

Professor Smith's "Universal Grammar of Religion" was first presented in March of 2005 as the fifth annual Venerable Hsüan Hua Memorial Lecture in Berkeley, California, and was subsequently published in the journal *Religion East & West*. With his participation and blessing, his Universal Grammar of religion is here re-presented in book form, by means of commentary, elaboration, and counterargument. His partner in this re-presentation is the philosopher Henry Rosemont, Jr., who was an MIT colleague of both Professor Smith and Professor Chomsky, and who himself had delivered a lecture in the Venerable Hsüan Hua Memorial series, with Professor Smith as respondent. For the present volume, Professor Rosemont has contributed an introduction, an initial response, a recorded discussion with Professor Smith, and a final reflection. In these he clarifies the Chomskyan theory of universal language structures. He both confirms and questions Professor Smith's application of the theory to religion, especially in the area of ontology. Finally, he identifies areas for further analysis for the next generation of scholar-practitioners of comparative religion.

— Martin J. Verhoeven
 General Editor, Venerable Hsüan Hua Memorial Lecture Series

— David Rounds
 Editor, *Religion East & West*

ACKNOWLEDGMENTS

Without the scholarly and editorial assistance of
Dr. Martin Verhoeven and David Rounds this volume
may well have never seen the light of published day.
I am deeply grateful to both of them for all their
assistance, and for their friendship as well. Ms. Lauren
Bausch worked long and hard on the transcriptions of
Huston's original lecture, my response, and our later
conversation; the basic substance, that is, of chapters
1, 2, and 3. She did a splendid job, which made my
editing and revising work much easier, and more
accurate, for which I am very grateful. Revamping
Huston's old typewritten diagram—a handout at his
lecture—into a legible visual asset suitable for printing
in this volume fell to the capable eyes and hands of
Mr. Loc Huynh, Ms. Stacy Chen, and Ms. Kristine Ang
Go, and the lexical research and translation of the
terms in the diagram was undertaken by Dr. Snjezana
Akpinar; for the high quality and clarity of the results
I thank them both. Bhikshu Heng Sure took the
photographs which grace the book, which aids

ACKNOWLEDGMENTS

measurably, I believe, in enhancing the personal quality of the work overall. And I am also grateful to my editor at Open Court, Ms. Cindy Pineo.

To all of these people, and all others affiliated with the Berkeley Buddhist Monastery, City of Ten Thousand Buddhas, and the Institute for World Religions I will be forever grateful; for their hospitality, intellectual companionship, and many other kind considerations toward myself over the past fifteen years.

— Henry Rosemont, Jr.

INTRODUCTION

*T*his is an unusual book, not least because it focuses largely on the ideas of the second author, but was basically written and put together by the first. Equally unusual, perhaps, is that the ideas of a third thinker—Noam Chomsky—loom large throughout the book, even though it deals primarily with the nature of religion, about which Chomsky has written virtually nothing.

When Huston Smith's original lecture and my response to it were being readied for publication in *Religion East & West* during the late summer of 2005, it became clear that together they were not sufficiently extensive for publication in the series of books that have been based on the Master Hsüan Hua Memorial Lectures. When asked by members of the IWR what might be done, I began to think of a joint effort between us, analogous to the collaborative work Huston did with David Ray Griffin in 1989, published under the title *Primordial Truth and Postmodern*

Theology.[1] Therein Griffin first gave a critique of Smith's "perennialist" position, followed by Smith's reply and critique of Griffin's postmodern stance. Griffin then penned a counter-reply, Smith a counter-rejoinder, and they then collaborated in writing an afterword.

It was an illuminating book, and I shall have more to say about some of Huston's views expressed in it, because some of them he has expressed again in these pages. But that dialogue was between two scholar/philosophers operating within the overarching framework of the Christian heritage, to which they both give allegiance, which is not the case in the present instance. I am not a Christian, do not believe in God or gods, am terrified at the possibility of surviving in any way the destruction of my body, and believe the idea of a transcendent realm is not only false, but mischievous, to the extent it causes us to lose sight of the splendor, majesty, and spiritual significance of this world—the only world I believe we will ever know.

Thus I knew the present work would differ in thrust, themes, and tone from the Smith-Griffin book (and from the other books in the Master Hsüan Hua Memorial Lecture Series, including my own). While Huston responded vigorously to Griffin's criticisms of his position—as intended—it seemed more important in the present case that I endeavor to have Huston

---

[1] David Ray Griffin and Huston Smith, *Primordial Truth and Postmodern Theology* (Albany, NY: SUNY Press, 1989).

elaborate the ideas that Chomsky's work had inspired in him, rather than simply criticize those ideas, especially when it is remembered that these are the latest and perhaps the culminating expression of the views of a scholar-practitioner approaching his eighty-ninth year on this planet.

At the same time, I agree with Huston that a number of Chomsky's views might fruitfully be applied to the study of religion and to the current debates surrounding religion. It also seemed incumbent on me to elaborate the Chomskyan position in some detail, so that readers might pick up the strands of the present arguments and weave them more closely together while yet enlarging what they might be capable of covering adequately.

The results of these concerns are now before the reader, in four chapters, beginning with a lengthier and revised version of Huston's lecture of March 2005, followed by a significantly expanded version of my response that same evening. These set the stage for the book's third chapter, a conversation between us in November 2006, which allowed Huston to elaborate on the views presented in the lecture. At the same time, the conversation allowed me to pose to him a few questions I am fairly sure had not been asked of him by other conversation partners in the past—including Bill Moyers's outstanding interviews with him[2]—but

---

[2] *The Wisdom of Faith with Huston Smith* (5-part VHS/DVD available from PBS).

which readers of Huston's works would profit from knowing.

This conversation did gather together all that Huston wished to say about his model of Chomskyan grammar in the field of religion, I believe, for in addition to parrying a few questions not recorded here, he was adamant that in order for the book to be a full-fledged dialogue between us, I should do less editorial and exegetical work, and instead write the final section of the book as a summation of my own views on the matters we had both been taking up; he had had his say, I should have mine.

Each of the four chapters begins with a brief foreword describing its genesis and subsequent modification. The important claims in each have been elaborated by the inclusion of notes and references to other works that bear on those claims.[3]

In his dialogues with Griffin, Huston, lamenting a seeming lack of direct engagement between them, wrote:

> I keep returning to my conviction that different visions, not arguments, regulate our conclusions; this is why we talk past each other so much, and why the issues between us are left, so often, unjoined.[4]

---

[3] All the endnotes and references are mine. I am grateful to Professor Martin Verhoeven for tracking down most of the references mentioned both in Huston's lecture and in my notes on Huston's lecture.

[4] Griffin and Smith, *Primordial Truth*, 158.

If this be so, it behooves the reader to gain some acquaintance with the differing visions represented in the present work, if the arguments it contains—on any side—are to have more than rhetorical force. My recommendation for background on Huston's vision would be his *Forgotten Truth: The Primordial Tradition*.[5] My own vision of religion is reflected in significant measure in my *Rationality and Religious Experience*,[6] in which Huston served as commentator. Having worked with Chomsky as student, junior colleague, fellow dissident, and cherished friend, I feel at least minimally confident of the accuracy of my account of his vision that bears on the themes of this book, but in addition to the citations to his writings to justify my interpretations, I would recommend, for a general account of the man and his work, either *Noam Chomsky: A Life of Dissent*[7] or *The Chomsky Update*.[8]

Finally, I am pleased to note that Huston has read the entire work just as readers have it before them, and endorsed it fully.

---

[5] Huston Smith, *Forgotten Truth: The Primordial Tradition* (New York: Harper & Row, 1977).

[6] Henry Rosemont, Jr., *Rationality and Religious Experience* (Chicago: Open Court, 2001).

[7] Robert F. Barsky, *Noam Chomsky: A Life of Dissent* (Cambridge, MA: MIT Press, 1997).

[8] Raphael Salkie, *The Chomsky Update* (London: Unwin Hyman, 1990).

Against this background we may proceed directly to the theme of this book, the question of there being a universal "grammar" of religion (and if so, what is it like?).

— Henry Rosemont, Jr.

Is There a
Universal Grammar
of Religion?

Henry Rosemont, Jr. (left) and Huston Smith (right), November 2006.

1
THE LECTURE
HUSTON SMITH

*The following differs from Huston Smith's original lecture
in two ways. First, he made a few minor changes as points
of clarification when he reviewed his original lecture for
publication in* Religion East & West *(Issue 5, October 2005).
Second, I have woven into the lecture several statements
Huston made in response to questions from the audience
following the lecture.—H.R.*

In his numerous original works in theoretical
linguistics, Noam Chomsky has described a "Universal
Grammar" that he believes is built into the human
mind and structures every human language. I had the
great good fortune to be a colleague of Chomsky's from
1958 to 1973 when we both taught at MIT (And it was
during the latter part of this period that I also had the
good fortune of meeting Henry Rosemont when, he,
too, came to MIT in 1969).

At the time, Chomsky's concept of Universal
Grammar was revolutionizing the study of linguistics,
but it was only very recently that I began to think the

concept might also be applicable to the study of religions, and that is the topic of this lecture.

The *Chandogya Upanishad* provides a nice entry into the project.

> As by knowing one lump of clay, all things made of clay
> are known, the difference being only in name and
> arising from speech, and the truth being that all are clay;
> as by knowing one nugget of gold, all things made of
> gold are known, the difference being only in name and
> arising from speech, and the truth being that all are
> gold—exactly so is that knowledge, by knowing which
> we know all. [1]

I have broken the clay/gold of religion into fourteen pieces, but before I list them, I should point out the background on which they are positioned. The world they describe is objective, in the sense that it was here before we were and it is our business to understand it. "Honor the object, not the subject," the poet Czeslaw Milosz admonished, and religion does that. [2]

This was taken for granted until modern philosophy introduced idealism as the opposite of realism. Science

---

[1] *Chandogya Upanishad*, chap. 4.1.4. The reader can refer to three translations of the Upanishads: an early rendition by F. Max Muller, *The Upanishads* (Oxford: Clarendon Press, 1879); a later version by R. S. Radhakrishnan, *The Principal Upanishads* (London: Allen Unwin, 1953); and, a more modern rendering by E. Easwaran, *The Upanishads* (Tomales, CA: Nilgiri Press, 1987).

[2] Czeslaw Milosz, *The Witness of Poetry* (Cambridge: Harvard University Press, 1983).

remains realistic because it can demonstrate what the world is like without us, but for the rest, modernity assumes that we must begin with how the world appears to us and extrapolate from there. William Blake noticed the mistake here. Once you begin with a self/world divide (as animals and traditional peoples do not) there is no way that Humpty Dumpty can put it back together again. As Blake wrote,

> The dim window of our soul
> Distorts the heavens from pole to pole
> And leads us to believe the lie
> That we see with, not thro', the eye. [3]

We see through windows, not with them.

That said, we can now proceed to enumerate the fixed points of the religious world:

1. Reality is infinite. The Infinite is the one inescapable metaphysical idea, for if you stop with finitude you face a door with only one side, which is an absurdity.

2. The Infinite includes the finite. Otherwise, we would be left with infinite plus finitude and the infinite would not be what it claims to be. The natural image

---

[3] *The Notebook of William Blake: Called the Rossetti Manuscript,* edited by Geoffrey Keynes (London: Nonesuch Press, 1935).

to token the Infinite's inclusiveness is a circle, for circles include more space than any other outline can. Out of the infinite, all-including circle, it is impossible for anything to fall. Augustine deified the Infinite Circle by saying that God is a circle whose center is everywhere and whose circumference is nowhere. (See my diagram on p. 13).

3. The contents of finitude are hierarchically ordered. Arthur Lovejoy titled his classic study in the history of philosophy *The Great Chain of Being,* and he argued that its underlying idea was accepted by most educated people throughout the world until modernity mistakenly abandoned it in the eighteenth century.[4] The "great chain of being" is the idea of a universe composed of an infinite number of links ranging in hierarchical order from the most meager kind of existence through every possible grade up to the boundless Infinite. The ascent may be a smooth continuum, but for practical purposes it helps to divide it into categories—steps on a ladder, so to speak. Aristotle's categories of mineral, vegetable, animal, and rational are a good start, but it ends too soon because we human beings—rational beings that we pride ourselves on being—are only halfway up the chain. Above them are heavenly choirs of angels, symbolized by Jacob's dream of angels ascending and descending

---

[4] Arthur O. Lovejoy, *The Great Chain of Being: A Study of the History of an Idea* (Cambridge: Harvard University Press, 2005).

on a ladder that reached from earth to heaven. In the third century, Origen inverted the ladder to point out that causation is from the top downward. All things started from one beginning, he said, but were distributed throughout the different ranks of existence in accordance with their merit; for in them goodness does not rest essentially, as it does in God.[5] For only in God, which is the source of all things, does goodness reside essentially. Others possess it as an accident, liable to be lost, and only then do they live in blessedness when they participate in holiness and wisdom and in the Divine nature itself.

4. Causation is from the top down. It extends from the Infinite down through descending degrees of reality. For three centuries science challenged this claim, but it is beginning to change its mind, and this change requires some commentary.

Science is empirical; everything within it, except for mathematics, spins off from our physical senses. The fact that those senses connect only with physical objects and that the entire house of science is founded on our physical senses has led scientists to assume that matter is the fundamental stuff of the universe. Their familiar scenario begins with the Big Bang which issued in the smallest conceivable entities—quarks,

------

[5] Origen's *Commentary on the Gospel of John 2* appears in *On First Principles*, translated by G. W. Butterworth (New York: Harper and Row, 1966).

strings, what have you—that progressively grouped themselves into progressively more complex entities until, in the latest nanosecond of cosmic time, life consciously emerged. It's upward causation all the way.

What is causing scientists to reconsider that scenario is their dawning realization that it contains no explanation for why complexity increases. To say that it rides the Big Bang's momentum is no good, for no one knows what powered the Big Bang in the first place. And to say that complex forms *emerged* fares no better, because "emerged" is a descriptive, not an explanatory concept.

All this is leading scientists to think that the foundational feature of the universe is not matter but information.[6] This changes the job of science, which scientists have assumed was to identify underlying structures that have to obey certain equations no matter what. Now, however, the world is seen as a hierarchy of nested systems—holons—that convey information, and the job of physical theory is to extract as much information from those systems as possible. This frees science from the reductionist project of forcing nature into its procrustean, empirical bed and turns scientists into inquirers who ask nature questions, obtaining answers and always remaining

---

[6] See Seth Lloyd, *Programming the Universe: A Quantum Computer Scientist Takes On the Cosmos* (New York : Alfred A. Knopf, 2006); and Michael A. Nielsen, "The Bits that Make Up the Universe, *Nature* 427:16–17 (01 Jan. 2004).

open to the possibility that nature has deeper levels to divulge. Nothing of substance in mechanist science is lost. The thing that does give way is that physics is a bottom-up affair in which knowledge of a system's parts determines knowledge of the system as a whole. In the informational approach the whole is invariably greater than the sum of its parts, which the religious worldview asserts in its top-down causation.

5. The One becomes the many. In descending to the finite, the singularity of the Infinite splays out into multiplicity. I know that a number of people would argue that the many are at all times present in the Infinite, or put another way, that it is relationship, not singularity, that is ultimate. But for myself, the parts of the many are virtues; they retain in lesser degree the signature of the Infinite, of the One's perfection at the top. The foundational virtue is existence; for to be more than figments of the imagination, virtues must exist. In the scholastic dictum, *esse qua esse bonum est*—"being as being is good." It is good simply to exist. As for what the virtues other than existence are, India begins with *sat, chat, ananda*—Being, consciousness, bliss. The West's ternary is the good, the true, and the beautiful, and these beginnings open out into creativity, compassion, and love until we arrive at Islam's Ninety-Nine Beautiful Names of God. The hundredth name on the Muslim rosary is absent because it is unutterable.

6. As virtues ascend the causal ladder, their distinctions fade and they begin to merge. We find that the drift of downward causation is reversed as we look upward from our position on the causal chain. This requires that we change Lovejoy's image of the ladder and chain and replace it with a pyramid. Teilhard de Chardin said that everything that rises must converge, and Flannery O'Connor adopted that for the title of one of her short stories.[7] (The saying is true. The longitudinal lines on our planet converge as

---

[7] Flannery O'Connor, *Everything That Rises Must Converge*, with an introduction by Hermione Lee (London: Faber, 1966). O'Connor took her short story title from a passage that appeared in the 1942 essay "The New Spirit" by the Jesuit geopaleontologist Pierre Teilhard de Chardin. His essay was later reprinted in the book *The Future of Man* (1969). Pierre Teilhard de Chardin (1881–1955) was a freethinker, visionary, and futurist who ran into trouble with the Catholic hierarchy for his unorthodox views as he attempted to reconcile theology with science, especially within an evolutionary perspective. He put forth a dynamic worldview in which he argued that the human species occupies a special place within a spiritual universe and that the ongoing spiritual evolution of our species is moving toward an Omega Point as the end-goal or divine destiny of human evolution on this planet. This Omega Point formed at the end of human evolution would be the climax of spiritual involution and divine convergence. His evolutionary optimism envisioned an evolving global mind in terms of love, spirit, information, and technology. Pierre Teilhard de Chardin served as director of the National Research Center of France, was a geology professor at the Catholic Institute in Paris, and directed the National Geologic Survey of China. He died in New York City in 1955.

they approach the north and south poles.) At the top of the pyramid God knows lovingly and loves knowingly, and so on, until (in the Infinite) differences, which symbolize separation, completely disappear in the divine simplicity. "Simplicity" here is a technical term; the idea can be likened to a mathematical point that has no extension. (There is nothing simple about a "simplicity" that includes everything. We might speak about distinctions without differences, but no amount of verbal legerdemain of that sort can do more than paper over the profound paradoxes when we try to understand God with our finite minds.) To refer to that point, any ontological virtue will serve as long as the word is capitalized, whereupon they all become synonyms. God is the conventional English for the Infinite, but the Good, the True, the Real, the Almighty, the One, and so on, are all equally appropriate.

7. At the top of the pyramid, absolute perfection reigns. To go back to the mathematical point, when power and goodness and the other virtues converge at the top of the pyramid, the religious worldview makes its most staggering claim, that of absolute perfection. This is indeed staggering, for it seems flatly contradicted daily with the horrors we read about in the morning newspaper. This is a conceptual headache, to put it mildly. But let's look at the matter logically.

I am personally comfortable with the word "God" to denote absolute perfection. We are here in the

Graduate Theological Union here in Berkeley, in a Christian chapel, and that is my heritage, so I am comfortable with the word "God." But I can translate it, I am confident, into any religious tradition if asked to do so. (Again, I refer to my diagram.)

God. In the beginning, God. Everything back to God. And God is perfect goodness and omnipotent, so just logically it seems as though that has to be the last word on the matter. So, despite the fact that the world is in about the worst shape imaginable, in the eye of the cyclone all is well, as Hegel put it.

Another way of looking at it is condensed in a Zen saying: "Snowflakes falling, flake by flake / Each flake falling in its proper place." Of course we must come face to face with the problem of evil. Human beings are capable of great nobility and horrendous evil. Our primary mistake is to put ourselves ahead of others. We cannot get rid of that error, but we must work to restrain it. We must remember that in the eyes of all the religions, the physical universe is transitory; it will come to an end at some point, but that doesn't mean it will be wiped out; it means that it will be redeemed, drawn back into the complete perfection of God. It's something like that—I've given an abbreviated form— that stands back of my very scandalous assertion, you might say. I do think it is true, and I think it is affirmed in different idioms by all the major religions, those which I have poured my life into trying to understand and which have had the greatest impact on history. Here is how I would describe my view in diagram form.

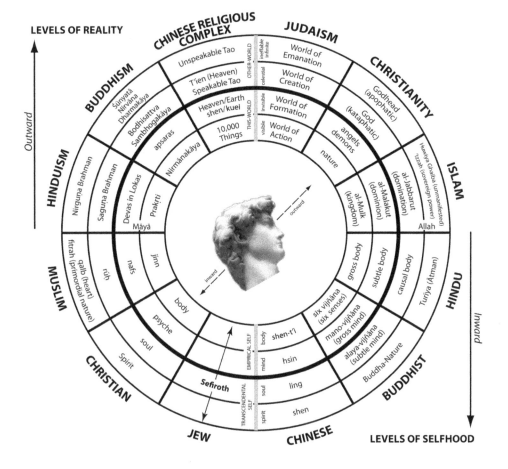

The diagram labeled "LEVELS OF REALITY" (top left) and "LEVELS OF SELFHOOD" (bottom right), with "Outward" and "Inward" axes, contains the following concentric labels across traditions:

CHINESE RELIGIOUS COMPLEX / JUDAISM / CHRISTIANITY / ISLAM / HINDU / BUDDHIST / CHINESE / JEW / CHRISTIAN / MUSLIM / HINDUISM / BUDDHISM

Chinese Religious Complex: Unspeakable Tao; T'ien (Heaven) Speakable Tao; Heaven/Earth shen/kuei; 10,000 Things

Judaism: OTHER-WORLD (ineffable/infinite) World of Emanation; celestial World of Creation; invisible World of Formation; THIS-WORLD / visible World of Action

Christianity: Godhead (apophatic); God (kataphatic); angels/demons; nature

Islam: Huwiya Ghaiba (unmanifested); 'Izzah (sovereign power); al-Jabbarut (domination); al-Malakut (dominion); al-Mulk (kingdom); Allah

Buddhism: Śūnyatā Nirvāna Dharmakāya; Bodhisattva Sambhogakāya; apsaras; Nirmānakāya

Hinduism: Nirguna Brahman; Saguna Brahman; Devas in Lokas; Prakṛti; Māyā

Inner circles (Levels of Selfhood):
Muslim: fitrah (primordial nature); qalb (heart); rūh; nafs; jinn; body
Christian: Spirit; soul; psyche; body
Jew: Sefiroth; TRANSCENDENTAL SELF / EMPIRICAL SELF; spirit soul mind body
Chinese: shen; ling; hsin; shen-t'i
Buddhist: Buddha-Nature; alaya-vijñāna (subtle mind); mano-vijñāna (gross mind); six vijñāna (six senses)
Hindu: Turīya (Ātman); causal body; subtle body; gross body

Center axis: outward / inward

(There is a glossary for this diagram in the back of the book.)

8. As above, so below. The Great Chain of Being—to return to Lovejoy's imagery—with its links that increase in worth, needs to be extended by the Hermetic Principle, "As above, so below." Everything that is outside is also inside us; "the Kingdom of God is within you." We intersect, inhabit, all the echelons of the chain of being. As Sir Thomas Browne recorded in his *Religio Medici*, "Man is a multiple amphibian, disposed to live, not only like other creatures in diverse elements, but in divided and distinguishable worlds."[8]

When we look out, it is natural to visualize the good as up. Angels invariably sing on high and gods live on the mountaintop. But when we look inward, the imagery flips and the best things lie deepest within us. The complete picture shows the ineffable, unutterable, *apophatic*—which is to say unspeakable—Godhead at the top, descending to the personal, describable, *cataphatic*—which is to say speakable—God, to angels, and from them down to the physical universe. But within us, value inverts and the divisions increase in worth. Mind is more important than body, our multiple souls more important than our mind, and Spirit, which is identical in us all, is more important than soul.

9. Human beings cannot fully know the Infinite. Intimations of it seep into us occasionally, but more than this we cannot manage on our own. If we are to know confidently, the Infinite must take the initiative

---

[8] Sir Thomas Browne, *Religio Medici* (1642), republished by Cambridge University Press, 1955. The *Religio Medici* is the apologia of a learned physician and devout Christian. He was member of the Church of England as established by Elizabeth I. Browne found no contradiction between religion and science. He held that religion reveals man's relation to God. Science is our partial knowledge of the laws of nature whereby the divine purpose is carried out in creation.

and show it to us through revelation. It has to be revealed to us, because there is no commensurability between the finite and the Infinite. Nature does the same thing by building this Universal Grammar of languages into our heads. We did not create that. It came from outside. To repeat what I said at the beginning, my ontological claims are that there is a world independent of us; that we are in the world; and that it is our business to try to understand the world. But I must underscore my belief that the world is there first, and there objectively.

10. Revelations have to be interpreted. Hence, we have the science of exegesis, which is the critical interpretation of religious appearances and texts, such as the Bible, to discover their intended meaning. These interpretations progress through four stages of ascending importance: the literal, the ethical, the allegorical, and the anagogic. First, the literal: what does the text explicitly assert?—Jesus was crucified, or the Buddha was enlightened under the Bodhi tree. Next, the ethical: What does the text explicitly tell us we should and should not do? Third, the allegorical meaning: Thomas and Jesus speaking in parables. Finally, and most important, the anagogic: What is the capacity of the text to inspire?

11. All these factors were once taken for granted. This changed with the rise of twentieth-century fundamentalism and the literalism it fixes on. It has generated so much confusion that it justifies a little excursus to indicate what the mistake was. And here science gives us a clue. Science has shown us that there are three great domains of size: the micro-world of infinitely small quantum mechanics; the macro-world that we live in where we measure distances by feet, yards, and miles; and the mega-world using ordinary language. You run into contradictions at every point, like these that cartographers run into when they try to depict the globe on the two-dimensional pages of a geography book. You can't do it accurately. Now, the Infinite, God, whatever you want to call him, her, or it—these pronouns never work—is at least as different from our everyday world as are quantum mechanics and relativity theory, for the sufficient reason that the Infinite includes both of those. Scientists recognize that their domain cannot be described in everyday language; still, we can get to their domain. We know about it from them, but they have to use their technical language, which is mathematics: numbers and equations. The same goes for religion. The only way we can access the upper levels of reality leading up to God is through our texts' technical language, which consists of symbols; and through our technical language, which consists of poetry, music, dance, art, and prose. Then we can get a grasp on God.

12. **There are two ways of knowing: the rational and the intuitive.** These two are distinct and complementary. The life and career of Blaise Pascal

throw them into exceptionally sharp relief. When he exclaimed what was to become his famous aphorism, "The heart has reasons the mind knows not of," the mind he was thinking of was his scientific mind, through which he achieved fame for his theory of probability in mathematics and his work on hydrodynamics in physics. And "heart" was his word for the organ through which burst the epiphany that turned his concern from science to religion. He wrote: "Fire! God of Abraham Isaac . . . Jacob. Not the philosophers and the learned . . . tears of joy . . . my God, let me not be separated from Thee forever."[9]

But that he never intended to dismiss philosophy and learning entirely is amply evidenced by his

---

[9] Blaise Pascal, *Pensées*; iv. 277. In *Pensées*, translated by A. J. Krailsheimer, reissue edition (New York: Penguin Classics, 1995). On November 23, 1654, Pascal is said to have been involved in an accident at the bridge at Neuilly. The horses plunged over the parapet and the carriage nearly followed them. Fortunately, the reins broke and the coach hung halfway over the edge. Pascal and his friends emerged unscathed, but the sensitive philosopher, terrified by the nearness of death, fainted away and remained unconscious for some time. Upon recovering fifteen days later, between ten thirty and twelve thirty at night, Pascal had an intense religious vision and immediately recorded the experience in a brief note to himself which began: "Fire. God of Abraham, God of Isaac, God of Jacob, not of the philosophers and the scholars. . . ." He concluded by quoting Psalm 119:16: "I will not forget thy word. Amen." He seems to have carefully sewn this document into his coat and always transferred it when he changed clothes; a servant discovered it only by chance after his death. Blaise Pascal, *Oeuvres complètes* (Paris: Seuil, 1960), 618.

eighteen closely reasoned *Lettres provinciales* in which he examined the fundamental problems of human existence, and by the fact that he chose the title *Pensées* for his entries into his notebook, in which he spelled out his conviction that the true function of reason is to attain the truth or supreme good.[10]

All of the religions of the world spell out the distinction between religion and intuition carefully.

---

[10] Editor's Note: The *Lettres provinciales* (Provincial letters) are a series of eighteen letters written by Pascal under the pseudonym Louis de Montalte. See, *Responses aux Lettres provinciales publiées par le secrétaire de Port-Royal contre les PP. de la Compagnie de Jésus, sur le sujet de la morale des dits Pères*. [An answer to the Provinciall letters published by the Jansenists, under the name of Lewis Montalt, against the doctrine of the Jesuits and school-divines made by some Fathers of the Society in France] (Printed at Paris: [s.n.], 1659). They are a defense of Jansenist Antoine Arnauld, a friend of Pascal's who in 1656 was condemned by the Faculté de Théologie at the Sorbonne in Paris for views that were claimed to be heretical. The first letter is dated January 23, 1656. The first few letters ridicule the dispute between the Thomists and the Jesuits on the nature of salvation; the rest of the letters are mainly an attack on Jesuit casuistry. Letter XVI contains the famous quote, "I would have written a shorter letter, but I did not have the time." Pascal's use of wit, humor, and mockery in attacking existing institutions made his work extremely popular and controversial. In 1660 Louis XIV banned the book and ordered it shredded and burned. Nevertheless, the letters survived and influenced the prose of later French writers like Voltaire and Jean-Jacques Rousseau. Said Voltaire concerning the greatness of the letters, "All types of eloquence are contained in these letters." See also Blaise Pascal, *Pensées and the Provincial Lettres*, Modern Library ed. (New York: Random House, 1941).

In the West, intellect (*intellectus, gnosis, sapentia*) is not reason (*ratio*); in Sanskrit, *buddhi* is not *manes*; in Islam *ma'rifah,* situated in the heart, is not *aql*, situated in the brain. In Hinduism, the knowledge that effects union with God is not discursive; it has the immediacy of direct vision, or sight.

13. Religions have outsides and insides. As walnuts have shells that house kernels, outer, exoteric forms house interior, esoteric cores. People differ in the way they relate to the two. The difference comes down to how adept they are with abstraction. Esoterics are comfortable with abstractions while exoterics need for ideas to be concrete and representational to be clear. It follows that exoterics like to think of the Infinite in personal terms, whereas esoterics, while subscribing to the idea of the Infinite-clothed-in-human-attributes, are at the same time aware of the danger that can easily turn into anthropomorphism, into making God too human. So exotericism it needs to be supplemented by esoterism. We need for God to be both like us—or we could not connect with him—but we also need God to be unlike us, because we cannot worship ourselves.

14. What we know is ringed about with darkness. Finally, it is a numinous darkness that lures, for we know that God sees it as light and at times we sense a kind of twilight zone around its edges. But to cognition the darkness remains. We are born in ignorance, we live in ignorance, and we die in ignorance. In relation to the infinite we stand as less than a simple protein in a single cell on a human finger. Though it is alive, that protein cannot know the cell in which it lives. How then can it conceive of the skin, the knuckle, or the finger's articulating joints, the intricacies of the ligaments, nerves, and muscles, the electro-biochemical process of that finger of which it is a negligible part? And even if it could contain all that understanding, it could never conceive of the whole hand of which it is a part that can find expression in the fingering of a guitar, the fist clenched in anger, the delicate touch needed for surgical repair of the heart. It is only a simple protein, an amino acid building block.

So much less are we in this mass of the universe and in the Infinite beyond it. Again, we are born in mystery, we live in mystery, and we die in mystery.

2
THE RESPONSE

HENRY ROSEMONT, JR.

Professor Smith's revised lecture does not dwell at length on the concept of Chomsky's Universal Grammar, but it does make the claim of the usefulness of Chomsky's ideas for the study of religion. My response to the lecture took up that theme (the response followed Smith's lecture in Religion East & West, *Issue 5, October 2005). Both lecture and original response presumed some familiarity with Chomsky's writings in linguistics, and I have therefore considerably revised and expanded the response herein in order to develop more fully some of the features of Chomsky's theory of Universal Grammar so that general readers may more clearly judge for themselves the appropriateness—or lack thereof—of taking the Chomskyan concept from the study of languages to the study of religions. Against this background, I then pursue in greater depth a few of my own views on religions that bear on Huston Smith's views, not only where we are in agreement, but equally on specific issues on which we may differ, and which therefore need to be explored in greater detail. Despite these many changes, I have attempted to retain the spirit and the style of the work as a response to the lecture.*

In his lecture Huston Smith has given us, as he always does, much to reflect upon. I believe it is fair to say there are "intimations of the infinite" in it, to use a phrase of his I will return to several times, and I therefore want to follow him on his tenth point, where he says that intimations of the infinite (and revelation as well) have to be interpreted, hence the science of exegesis, which is how this response will be best read.

I will begin by spelling out, in general terms, a number of the features of Chomsky's theory of Universal Grammar which are, in my opinion, altogether appropriate as a template for the study and appreciation of religion and of religious experience. Huston has long demonstrated a particular genius for finding analogies that illuminate, usually in comparative perspective, dimensions of religion and religious experience that are of value to students, scholars, adherents, and adepts alike. There are, however, some other features of Chomsky's Universal Grammar which do not, in my opinion, fit well with Huston Smith's account. I want to quickly sketch these features, too, and then proffer some suggestions for interpreting Smith's views so that they may indeed fit with more of the dimensions of the Chomskyan linguistic vision, and hence answer affirmatively the question, Is there a Universal Grammar of religion? Of course the analogy cannot be pressed too far. Linguistic experience and religious experience are very different, to the extent that some scholars of religion even deny that the expression "religious experience" is meaningful, which no one would be inclined to say of the world of language.

It may strike some readers as odd that Huston Smith entitled his lecture by reference to the theoretical work of Noam Chomsky, and then began it with a quotation from the *Chandogya Upanishad.* Both references, however, and their juxtaposition, are in my opinion altogether apt. Just as the latter claims one lump of clay can suffice for knowing the essentials of clay, so, too has Chomsky always insisted that many of the principles of Universal Grammar could be discovered by a close examination of a single language—preferably the investigator's own—be the language English, Russian, Walpiri, or Urdu.

Chomsky's reasoning is straightforward: if there are principles that speakers of a language or dialect demonstrably follow from childhood on, but that were not or could not have been learned solely on the basis of direct linguistic experience or tutoring, then those principles must form part of the cognitive endowment that all normal human beings bring to bear in acquiring their native tongue. And it is the task of theoretical generative linguists to formulate hypotheses about what those highly abstract principles might be, and then "test" those hypotheses by observing linguistic behavior (which might be their own, with the observations introspective).

Chomsky has regularly referred to this phenomenon, and consequent research orientation, as "Plato's Problem."[1] How is it that in a number of cognitive domains we come to know a great deal on the basis of a miniscule amount of empirical data, and that much of what we know in these domains is not directly given in the data? To take a simple illustration from English, consider how we transform indicative sentences to interrogative "yes-no" questions. That is, how do we go from

1. The boy is reading a book.

to

2. Is the boy reading a book?

The easiest solution is to form a rule which, niceties aside, says to take the first occurrence of a verbal auxiliary in the indicative sentence and move it to the beginning of the sentence. This is indeed an easy rule, and it will work with more complex sentences as well:

3. The boy at the table is reading a book.

becomes

4. Is the boy at the table reading a book?

---

[1] Noam Chomsky, *Knowledge of Language* (New York: Praeger, 1986), xxv, for example. Note that while Universal Grammar is indeed a theory, Generative Grammar more generally is not, according to Chomsky; it is a topic for study (4). The research orientation for dealing with "Plato's problem" he calls the "Galilean style," about which, more below.

If, however, we take a fully relativized sentence, our simple and concrete "rule" won't work. The sentence

   5. The boy who is sitting at the table is reading a book.

would become

   *6. Is the boy who sitting at the table is reading a book?

which is ungrammatical. Clearly a different rule is needed, and the one that works for English is: take the first occurrence of a verbal auxiliary that occurs after the noun phrase structure and move it to the beginning of the sentence. This rule will correctly generate not only (2) and (4), but (7) as well:

   7. Is the boy who is sitting at the table reading a book?

This kind of knowledge is so simple and straightforward that not a few social scientists—in some cases, continuing to this day—have wondered why Chomsky would make such a fuss over this and similar phenomena that every normal seven-year-old native speaker of English will know. But for Chomsky, the interesting scientific question is how we come to learn such things at such an early age with virtually no explicit instruction (Does anyone remember their parents giving them the rule for forming "yes-no" questions in English?), Even more importantly, he has asked how we can come to know this or any other proposed principle of Universal Grammar that operates abstractly on *structures not directly given in experience*. Only the *order* of words is given in experience (first-last, left-right) not the *structures* of the sentences those words form (noun phrase, verb phrase, prepositional phrase, etc.).

Thus, although Chomsky has called this abstract syntactic schema "Universal Grammar,"[2] the name can be misleading at first blush, especially if it is taken to mean "grammatical rules or principles which are uniform throughout the universe," which suggest that alien forms of communication would exhibit them no less than human languages. Such is not at all what he means. Rather has he devoted his professional life as a theoretical linguist to studying the specific mental structures by means of which all normal human beings come to be competent speakers of their native language or dialect fairly independently of intelligence or motivation, with minimal and frequent degenerate inputs, and with virtually no formal instruction. Chomsky seeks, in other words, not rules or principles which hold "throughout the universe," but what I have called "homoversal" principles, a neologism meaning "for all human beings, mentally and physiologically constituted as they are," and consequently my own preference would be to use the expression

---

[2] At least since 1968: Noam Chomsky, *Language and Mind*, 1st ed. (New York: Harcourt, Brace, and World), 76.

"Homoversal Grammar of Religion" in our discussions. I believe Chomsky would agree with my use of "homoversal" as the referent for linguistic principles, but "Universal Grammar" is the coin of the realm today, and there is no harm in employing it so long as its proper domain is understood.

In addition to a language-capacity mental structure, that is, Universal Grammar, Chomsky has postulated similar specific mental capacities, or modules, embodying principles in music, personality discrimination, mathematics, facial recognition, and other areas where human beings seem to behave quite skillfully and similarly in areas where they have been exposed to little empirical data that could account for how the skill was acquired and uniformly exhibited in virtually the same way by everyone across time, space, and culture[3]—that is, more instances of "Plato's Problem." In other writings I have extended the Chomskyan model of the human mind to the field of ethics and aesthetics, claiming that here, too, we can find evidence of homoversal principles holding for all human beings, mentally and physiologically constituted as they are.[4] And I believe that is

---

[3] Noam Chomsky, *Reflections on Language* (New York: Pantheon Books, 1975), 21.

[4] For a more detailed discussion of homoversal principles as I define the concept, see my "Against Relativism," in *Interpreting Across Boundaries*, edited by Gerald Larson and Eliot Deutsch (Princeton: Princeton University Press, 1987).

exactly what Huston Smith is doing for the field of religion.

To get clearer on the appropriateness of the analogy as I see it, let's return to common features of English. As we have already noted, the "yes-no" question-formation rule operates on structure, not order. So does every other rule, or principle, of English and all other human natural languages. For another simple example, consider the following sentences:

> 8. Slowly the boy walked up the hill.
> *9. The slowly boy walked up the hill.
> 10. The boy slowly walked up the hill.
> 11. The boy walked slowly up the hill.
> *12. The boy walked up slowly the hill.
> *13. The boy walked up the slowly hill.
> 14. The boy walked up the hill slowly.

What is it about (9), (12), and (13) that make them ungrammatical while the others are not? The answer is that the adverb "slowly" is placed within a structure in these starred sentences, violating the integrity of those structures. The overall pattern of the sentence—as with a great many sentences in English—is noun phrase ("the boy"), verb phrase ("walked"), and prepositional phrase ("up the hill"). The adverb may be placed before or after any of these structures (8, 10, 11, 14), but not *within* any of them.

Very interesting, it might now be thought, but what do these details of Chomskyan theory (or the English language) have to do with *religion* or the study thereof?

In the first place, just as all human societies have abstract underlying principles governing the languages spoken in them, so also do their religions and religious practices—which is not as simplistic a generalization as it may initially appear when it is remembered and emphasized, again, that the underlying principles of Universal Grammar are *not directly given* in experience.[5] In just the same way, what Smith calls— and, I would suggest, we all understand him— "intimations of the infinite" are not directly given in experience either; yet, unless suffering from a kind of religious aphasia, almost everyone has had such experiences, across time, space, and culture.

Relatedly, even though the structure-dependence rule of Universal Grammar holds for all human languages, it is by no means clear that it aids communication—order-dependence would be far simpler and more straightforward, and surely more easily teachable. Hence the generalization that the primary function of language is to communicate might be questioned (as Chomsky has done),[6] and hence

---

[5] I have discussed the significance of this claim in Henry Rosemont, Jr., "Gathering Evidence for Linguistic Innateness," *Synthese* 38 (1978).

[6] He has held this view for most if not all of his career. I first came across it in Noam Chomsky, *Current Issues in Linguistic Theory* (Amsterdam: Mouton, 1964), 202–5. He has a lengthier account in Chomsky, *Reflections on Language,* 56–73, and I have taken up the issue in Rosemont, "Gathering Evidence for Linguistic Innateness."

in turn we might question the generalization that language use provided a strong selectional advantage to *homo sapiens*.

Here I must be careful, both on Chomsky's behalf and my own. To express skepticism of the claim that the human capacity for language developed because, in evolutionary terms, it conferred a selectional advantage on the species, is not at all to renounce Darwin or provide any aid or comfort to proponents of the vacuous notion of "intelligent design." Rather it is to claim, on the generative theory of linguistics, that there are certain features of the human language capacity that do not appear to aid communication in any way, or, in other cases, cannot be used at all because of interference from other mental capacities or the lack of an efficient parser.[7] We simply have these

---

[7] It might be well to let Chomsky speak for himself on these most important, if initially counterintuitive, claims. One recent account: "In fact, the system is 'inefficient,' in the sense that large parts of the language—even short and simple expressions—are unusable, though they have quite definite sound and meaning, determined by the generative procedure of the language faculty. The language is simply not well adapted to parsing. In the background there is a familiar fairy tale sometimes called 'Darwinism' that probably would have shocked Darwin: that the systems of the body are well adapted to their functions, perhaps superbly so. What this is supposed to mean is unclear. It is no principle of biology. On some interpretations, the statement just seems false. Nothing follows about the theory of evolution, which in no way suggests that the systems that have developed should be well adapted to conditions of life." *Powers and Prospects* (Boston: South End Press, 1996), 15.

features as part of our natural endowment, in the same way that most hawks have black underfeathers despite the lack of hunting advantage such coloration gives the predator when aloft.

In the same way, Smith is claiming, if I understand him aright, that human beings have a "capacity" to have intimations of the infinite, to apprehend what is beyond or behind our normal sensory experiences. And the evidence for this claim can be found in the sacred texts and practices of all of the world's religions, distant from each other in time and space. I believe Smith would call these intimations "religious experiences," and I would call them that, too, despite the arguments of many reductionists in the field of religious studies, who have departed from the stance of William James in the study of religion in a way that Smith has not. Near the close of *The Varieties of Religious Experience*, James makes the following autobiographical comment:

> I *can*, of course, put myself into the sectarian scientist's attitude, and imagine vividly that the world of sensations and scientific laws and objects may be all. But whenever I do this, I hear that inward monitor of which W. K. Clifford once wrote, whispering the word 'bosh!' Humbug is humbug, even though it bear the scientific name, and the total expression of human experience, as I view it objectively, invincibly urges me beyond the narrow 'scientific' bounds.[8]

---

[8] William James, *The Varieties of Religious Experience* (New York: Mentor Books, 1960), 391; italics in the original.

Just as we simply "have" the principle of structure dependence as part of our mental equipment without it seeming to confer any selectional advantage on the species, so, too, do we appear to "have" a capacity for experiencing the infinite; yet it would be folly, in my opinion, to attempt to explain this phenomenon in Darwinian terms. (Moreover, even if it did explain the phenomena in terms of selection, that would tell us nothing about the experience itself, either terms of its source, form, or content). I shall say more about the concept of religious experience below, but first want to note still a third feature of Chomsky's Universal Grammar that Smith can apply to religion, namely, that you can learn much about common features of both languages and religions by studying a single example of each.

The structure-dependence principle of Universal Grammar, we have already emphasized, is not directly given in experience. It is also noteworthy that we come to employ it and other principles of Universal Grammar despite the fact that some of the linguistic data we do experience is degenerate, in the sense of not being grammatical. Being angry, forgetful, interrupted, and the like, regularly causes people to speak in sentence fragments, but children hearing these fragments—and they are spoken frequently by almost everyone—do not imitate them, but seem to ignore the "bad data" without being told to do so. Once, to use a personal example of many years ago when my daughters were young, I was preparing spaghetti for dinner, and rummaging unsuccessfully through the spice cabinet for the oregano, and called out to my wife, "Dear, where did you put the—Oh never mind, I found it." Such speech is by no means uncommon in any household, and yet we do not tell our children, highly impressionable though they are in most other respects, to ignore the ungrammatical sentences we speak; indeed, we usually are not even consciously aware of these grammatical lapses. Moreover, it is clear that neither structure dependence nor any other principle of Universal Grammar is normally taught to native speakers of English when they are young; apart from professional linguists, very few adults can even articulate the principles they follow without reflection, just as they do not reflect on their linguistic lapses.

From these facts it must follow that structure dependence and other principles of Universal Grammar must be innate in the human mind,[9] and—unlike the principles and rules of physics, chess, or geology, which must be formally taught—these principles are uniform throughout the species, not for English speakers alone, yet they can be ascertained just from the study of English (or any other natural language).[10] It must follow in turn that all human

---

[9] As with most of these references, they have numerous sources in Chomsky's numerous writings over the years. One such in the present instance is *Rules and Representations*, 45.

[10] For discussion, see Rosemont, "Gathering Evidence for Linguistic Innateness."

natural languages will exhibit these principles despite their being applied in different ways in different languages: in English, modifying adjectives generally precede their noun in the noun phrase structure (the red cars); in French, they generally follow their noun (*les autos rouges*).

Hence we can see one significant dimension of the parallel I believe Smith is attempting to draw between (the study of) linguistics and (the study of) religion, for I am confident he would agree that the fourteen points of his metaphysical vision can be derived from the careful study of a single faith tradition, which must be why he used the *Chandogya Upanishad*'s lump of clay example as he did. My own acquaintance with the many and varied sacred texts is not on a par with Smith's, but none of those with which I am familiar are incompatible with the thrust of the account of the religious impulse he has given in his lecture.

This point will be difficult to appreciate for students of religion who concentrate on the theologies and cosmologies of the world's religions, for these are wildly inconsistent not only with each other, but with the findings of modern science as well (a point on which Smith and I might be in disagreement, a topic to be returned to below). But differing cosmologies and theologies no more vitiate his claim for a universal or homoversal "grammar" of religion than the radically different features of different natural languages like English, Hungarian, Japanese, or Hopi in any way challenge Chomsky's theory of a Universal Grammar

descriptive of all human natural languages. Religious
cosmologies are here metaphysical or theological,
there analogic or metaphorical; here influenced by
geography and climate, there clearly by language
and accidents of history. It is physical geography that
explains why African sculptors worked in wood while
their Italian Renaissance counterparts chiseled marble.
At the same time we need culture and history to
explain why, although marble is as common in China
as in Italy, Chinese sculptors would carve a Guan Yin,
not a pieta.

But to my mind the African, Italian, and Chinese
carver/sculptors were all simply expressing, in a
concrete physical medium, their stance and reaction
to the universe *qua* universe, to the intimations of
mortality and of the infinite they experienced, and
their works will be better understood and appreciated
by appealing to the principles of religious "grammar"
that Smith's lecture explicates as definitive, again, of
all human beings, physiologically and mentally
constituted as they are.

I believe the diagram that Smith has given us here
(see page 13) begins to flesh out his idea of this
"grammar" of religion on the basis of the conclusions
he has drawn from his decades-long study of the major
religions of the world in comparative perspective.
The diagram looks outward and "upward" toward the
heavens; it also looks inward and "downward" as
Smith says, to that which "lies deepest within us." He
finds four similar "chains of being" in each tradition—

material, invisible, celestial, and the infinite or ineffable—when we reach up and outward as one of the arrows emanating from the eye of the contemplative religious person in the diagram shows. Parallel to this upward orientation, the other arrow points us inward to four other "chains of being"—body, mind, soul, and spirit—that we encounter as we explore ourselves in depth inwardly (as described in Smith's eighth point.)

Some scholars will undoubtedly criticize Smith's schematization as too neat and tidy, forcing much too much that is disparate in each of the world's religious heritages into the same procrustean boxes. I, too, would cavil at some of the juxtapositions, but I believe that a great many of the similarities he has found in his studies are there to be found, provided that one looks at the deeper structures underlying the religions that his diagram endeavors to portray (if I am interpreting him correctly on this score)—rather than looking at their surface structures, such as rituals, myths, legends, practices. I agree that these underlying similarities are too striking to be dismissed as coincidences. And when we speak of the differences between "surface" and "deep" or "underlying" structures, we are, of course, operating within the overall conceptual framework in which Chomsky has revolutionized the study of linguistics.

Against this background I would like to turn for a while from linguistics and religion to Huston Smith as author of this lecture. I am in the first instance curious—as I am sure many of his listeners and readers are—about how much of the vision and insight presented in this lecture is based on his experiences as a practitioner of a multiplicity of spiritual disciplines in a wide variety of faith traditions, and how much is based on his professional life as a scholar/philosopher of religions and their sacred texts—appreciating fully that the distinction almost surely should not be drawn as sharply as I have just done.

I suspect strongly that the answer is not either/or but both/and. To the extent that his spiritual principles are derived from a religious experience, or from a series of them—even if they were derived from spiritual practices within a single faith—the principles might well be construed at least in part as absolutely general. We need not see them as uniquely Christian, nor as merely autobiographical; they do not merely tell us something about Huston Smith and his faith tradition, any more than the principles of Universal Grammar merely tell us something about English.

If, moreover, Smith has had a multiplicity of religious experiences resulting from deeply immersing himself—which I know he has done—in a number of spiritual disciplines in a variety of the world's religions, then his lecture begins to illuminate even less the personal odyssey of Huston Smith, and much more what we might call, analogous to our Chomskyan language capacity, a homoversal "spiritual capacity" in all human beings, mentally and physiologically constituted as they are.

This possibility of a "Universal Grammar of religion" becomes all the more intriguing to contemplate when we turn from practitioner Smith to Professor Smith, who has taught the sacred texts of the world's religions to generations of students, and whose book on the subject has sold almost two million copies worldwide. His book has done much, in my view, to cure the religious bigotry infecting the peoples of differing faith traditions, despite the large amount of it that unfortunately remains. Those two million copies, and the tolerance they have engendered, were sold largely, I think, because of the simple question the author asked of each religion, and especially of its belief system and practices: how could an intelligent, decent human being believe such things, and engage in such practices?

Huston Smith, almost alone in the field of comparative religious scholarship, gave intelligent and sensitive answers to the question for every one of the world's major faiths. If he had done nothing else, we would all still be deeply in his debt for the manifold contributions to human understanding of the "other" he has given us.

For myself, however few or many religious experiences Smith may have had, I admire the scholarly analytic skills he has combined with deep sensitivity to see beyond the specific cultural features embedded in each religion's sacred texts, rituals, symbols, liturgies, myths, and legends, in order to describe in more general terms a decidedly human orientation toward the world. He has, throughout his life, described this orientation in almost all of his writings, in *Forgotten Truth* and *Beyond the Post-Modern Mind* no less than in *The World's Religions.*[11]

In all of this work a cross-cultural approach has been central. As he said in his lecture, "'God' is the conventional English name for the Infinite, but 'the Good,' 'the True,' 'the Real,' 'the Almighty,' 'the One,' etc., are equally accurate" (with or without capitals, I would add, although he urges them). And of course there are many other names, in many other languages, for the referent of our spiritual sense, called the "Infinite" in the West largely because, in my view, of the peculiar development of mathematics in the Western intellectual world early on, beginning with Pythagoras. Of course Smith knows well many of these other names too, from *Nirguna Brahman* to *Śūnyatā* to *Dao*. In affirming these names no less than his own name "God" from his Methodist faith for as long and as resolutely as he has done, he suggests a sense of our co-humanity across time, space, language, and culture, a sense of our co-humanity on a par with our sense of awe in our intimations of the infinite.

Now if my interpretations of what Huston Smith has said and done, in his lecture and in almost all of his other work, is warranted, it follows, I believe, that much of the significance of what he has said and written will be lost if we concentrate on asking whether

---

[11] All first published by Harper & Row (New York), in 1976, 1982, and 1958 respectively. (The latter was originally entitled *The Religions of Man.*)

his ontological pronouncements—as many of them
appear to be—are literally true of the physical
universe. On this point he and I really seem to differ,
and a part of the difference lies in my taking Chomsky's
views even farther than Huston is willing to do.

At the end of his lecture Smith uses the word
"mystery" to characterize much of our human life, and
he used the word "ignorance" immediately beforehand
to similarly describe an essential ingredient of the
human condition. Chomsky does the same, sharply
distinguishing "problems"—which he believes the
human cognitive capacity overall is capable of
solving—and "mysteries," which probably lie beyond
our human ken. For Chomsky, problems may be clearly
formulated, and we have theories to guide our research
in seeking hypotheses to solve them. As he says:

> We can distinguish in principle between "problems,"
> which lie within [our intellectual capacities] and can be
> approached by human science with some hope of
> success, and what we might call "mysteries," questions
> that simply lie beyond the reach of our minds, structured
> and organized as they are. . . .[12]

Thus a "problem" in generative linguistics might be
why the sentence

---

[12] See Chomsky, *Reflections on Language*, 137–39; Noam
Chomsky, *Language and Thought* (New York: Moyer Bell, 1993),
53; and Noam Chomsky, *New Horizons in the Study of Language
and Mind* (Cambridge: Cambridge University Press, 2000), 133.

15. "John is too unusual to understand."

changes significantly in meaning when "it" is appended
thereto:

16. "John is too unusual to understand it."

but,

17. "This book is too unusual to understand
    without reading."

does not:

18. "This book is too unusual to understand
    without reading it."

—means exactly what (17) means.

Chomskyan "mysteries" are rather different. For
him there is no way to clearly formulate the problem,
no theory to guide research in solving it, not even a
clue as to what a proper solution might look like. We
simply see the phenomenon, and stand in awe of the
mysteriousness of it.[13] Chomsky's cardinal example of
such a mystery has always been what he has referred
to as the "creative use" of language by all normal
language users.[14] What makes this use creative, for

---

[13] This strong version of the claim about mysteries is mine;
Chomsky is a bit more circumspect. See the sources cited in the
prior two notes.

[14] See "Psychology and Ideology" in Chomsky's *For Reasons of
State* (New York: Vintage Books, 1973). And in Chomsky, *Rules and*

Chomsky, is that we can, and regularly do, respond to external stimuli in ways that are fully appropriate to the environmental situation, but are not *determined* by it. Given any environmental stimuli, there are an indefinitely large number of verbal responses that might appropriately be made to it, and for Chomsky, this is the *normal* use of language.

He has been making this point since his 1957 review of B. F. Skinner's *Verbal Behavior*,[15] in which he pointed out that "beautiful," for example, is not the only response that can be made to seeing the Mona Lisa. "Why is she smiling like that?" "What an ugly frame!" "It clashes with the wallpaper" "Why is this painting so famous?"—and countless other things could be said in response to this single external environmental stimulus, all of them influenced by the stimulus, and appropriate in response to it, but not determined thereby.

Why? What might explain the wellsprings of human motivation and behavior in this or many other similar situations? Chomsky's belief is that while some other form of intelligence might be able to answer such questions about human beings, human beings themselves cannot do so. To be sure, we can learn much more about human beings than we currently

---

Representations, 222: "The study of grammar raises problems that we have some hope of solving; the creative use of language is a mystery that eludes our grasp."

[15] Reprinted in *The Structure of Language*, edited by Jerry Fodor and Jerrold Katz (New Jersey: Prentice-Hall, 1964), 547–78.

know, but many of the central features of our humanity must lie beyond our ken, and for Chomsky these features will almost surely remain mysteries to us.[16] As in much else, I support him fully in this. For instance, a full science of human beings would require the subscience of human cognitive capacity, which would have to include statements about what lies beyond human cognitive capacity. But it is a tautology to say that what lies beyond human cognitive capacity lies beyond human cognitive capacity. Cognitive science has come a long way in the past half-century, and will undoubtedly continue to develop in productive ways. But a full subscience of human cognitive capacity is not possible for human beings, it seems to me; hence in turn no science of human beings is possible for human beings. There are many problems for human scientists to work on, but the mysteries will always with us, and our successors as well.

Huston Smith, however, places the mystery more outside the human realm, I think, than either Chomsky or I would do, even though he makes clear in his fourth point that all our knowledge of the physical world, apart from mathematics, comes through our senses. And as Smith says at the outset of his lecture, "Modernity . . . assumes that we must begin with how the world *appears* to us and extrapolate from there." My own view, and I suspect Chomsky's as well, is more or less Kantian on this score: that is, the appearances

---

[16] See Chomsky, *Rules and Representations*, 33ff. and note 13 above.

are all that we will ever have, and so ontological statements that go beyond them, except at the level of common sense, must remain speculative, concerns of faith undoubtedly, but not of science, nor of knowledge. The color spectrum, for example, runs from infrared to ultraviolet, but this is not, to my way of thinking, a statement about the way the universe is. Rather are correct statements about the spectrum, I would suggest, to be seen as faithful to the powers and limitations of the human language capacity and of the visual sensory organ to see and refer to colors within it, beyond which boundaries on either end we have a single term: "black." The same may be said for what is audible with our aural sensory organ. Further, the way nouns, verbs, modifiers, and other elements of linguistic structures can and cannot interact with each other are not in any sense true of the universe— necessary for any form of communication anywhere— but statements of the principles of Universal Grammar can be read as faithful to the way human beings think about and communicate their visual, auditory, olfactory, and other sensations homoversally, mentally, and physiologically constituted as they are.

I am not certain that Chomsky would concur with this way of looking at the matter, but he might, for he has long held that the set of sciences and theories accessible to human beings is fairly limited.[17] For myself, I would hold that while there may indeed be

---

[17] Chomsky, *Rules and Representations*, 6–7, 46, 252.

a true theory of the universe, it would be the height of anthropomorphic arrogance to believe that human beings were uniquely equipped to ascertain what that theory might be, given the particular organs we have for sensing a part of the external world, and the means we have for communicating what has been sensed. It may take intelligent life forms very, very different from our own to perceive the constituents of the universe as they "really" are, and clearly the language these life forms would employ to correctly describe the universe would be unintelligible to us.

If this be so, then I can only repeat my earlier suggestion to listeners and readers of Huston Smith's text not to ask whether or not the metaphysical statements in his lecture are literally true, but rather to see them as endeavoring to be faithful to a distinctively human stance in reaction and relation to, and cognizant of, what I join him in referring to as the "Infinite." That is to say, I want to interpret the lecture as his account of this human stance as he has come to understand and apprehend it, as reflected in the spiritual disciplines he has practiced, and in the sacred texts he has studied over the course of an exceptionally long and rich intellectual and spiritual journey.

But I suspect that Smith will want to say he intends more than the human dimension. He wants to speak directly about the ultimate reality beyond the world of appearances; he wants to say, I think, that the great chain of being, as described by Lovejoy (Smith's eighth point) is not just a human effort to put into words differing kinds of spiritual responses to religious experiences in the West—Lovejoy's focus—but is somehow a true statement about the universe. And it is difficult not to read him this way because of the way he weaves science in and out of his narrative.

To a significant extent I am here attempting to carry on a dialogue that Huston Smith and I entered into seven years ago, when our roles were reversed: I was the Hsüan Hua Memorial Lecturer and he was my commentator.[18] Much of my lecture was devoted to claiming that the sacred texts of the world's religions all provided spiritual disciplines for the achievement of religious experiences which I described as a strong feeling of belonging, or of attunement, or, in Wittgenstein's Christian-flavored account, "the experience of being *absolutely safe*."[19] Throughout my lecture I eschewed discussing the cosmologies to be found in those texts, except to say that no one knowledgeable about science in the twenty-first century could give any of them any credence. In concluding his incisive commentary, Smith had this to say:

> I really liked what you moved up to in the notion of the mystical, absolute safety, and the notion of belonging.

---

[18] Published as *Rationality and Religious Experience* (Chicago: Open Court, 2001).

[19] "Wittgenstein's Lecture on Ethics," *Philosophical Review* 74 (1965): 8; italics in the original.

But again, are these simply psychological states that these traditions give us as directives for how we can come to these feelings? Or, do they dig deeper into the nature of things to describe a reality, the ultimate reality which gives grounds for us to think that we are not just making it up when we have these sentiments of safety and belonging?[20]

I responded as best I could at the time, and amplified my answer to some extent in the little book which resulted from our exchange and from my exchanges with the audience. But one important dimension of my claim did not get presented there, for it was linguistically inspired, and I didn't mention Chomsky at all in that lecture. My claim would be that just as we are "hard-wired" to respond in certain ways to human speech—the Universal Grammar—so are we wired equally to feel a sense of belonging in the natural world we experience with our sensory organs. But beyond that I make no ontological commitments, in the same way I do not want to say that nouns, verbs, or linguistic structures of any kind are "out there" apart from human mental organs. Nor would I argue that such a religious response to our environment is or is not in any way adaptive for the species; we just have this capacity for response, that's all. My evidence for this claim is the sacred texts and commentaries of the world's religions, and the writings of adepts in each

---

[20] *Rationality and Religious Experience*, 40.

tradition. All of them seem to be saying virtually the same thing, as I read them.[21] And they have been saying the same thing the world over, over the span of at least four thousand years, from within very different cultural and linguistic communities. Much of what Huston Smith describes in his fourteen points, and in his diagram, synthesizes much of what I have read, which is why I have endorsed for the most part his adapting Chomsky's theory of human language to religion.

In this way, although I restrict myself to the human realm, I take that realm, and religious experience, very seriously, and do not believe we are somehow "just making it up." But as his remarks both then and now suggest, Smith does seem to want to say more, as he does at the outset of his lecture:

> The world [that my fourteen points] describe is objective, in the sense that it was here before we were and it is our business to understand it.

He reiterates this claim in his ninth point:

> Nature does the same thing by building this Universal Grammar of language into our heads. We did not create that. It came from outside.

Now if by "outside" Smith means that our linguistic capacity is not such that we can modify it

---

[21] As argued at length in *Rationality and Religious Experience*, especially pp. 24–34.

at will—that it does not depend on our whim, or even on any particular psychological state—then I would heartily agree, and believe Chomsky would as well. Language is simply an important feature of the species *homo sapiens*, and I would say the same for the religious capacity. But if by "outside" Smith wants to go beyond human biology, I fear I may not be able to join him.

At the same time, I must confess uncertainty about my reading of him on this score. Many years ago he and I were on a panel together either at the American Academy of Religion or American Philosophical Association annual meeting, at which he gave a brilliant presentation on the concept of truth, in which he claimed that the concept referred primarily to reality in the Indian tradition ("true north" is one of the very few Western examples) and to human relations in the Chinese tradition ("true friend"), and served as a predicate of statements in the Greek and later Western tradition. ("The statement 'grass is green' is true").[22] Hence perhaps Smith is claiming that religious truth is to be interpreted more in the Indian than in the Western sense of the term. This is one way of construing his references to Pascal in his twelfth point,

---

[22] His presentation was later published under the title "Western and Comparative Perspectives on Truth," *Philosophy & East* 30, no. 4 (October, 1980), and reprinted as "Truth in Comparative Perspective" in *Huston Smith: Essays On World Religion*, edited by M. Darrol Bryant (New York: Paragon House, 1992).

namely, that religious experiences are as much—if not more—matters of the heart as of the head. But putting the matter in this way exhibits a Western bias that Smith's youth spent in China would make him question. In Chinese, the same word signifies both the seat of thought and the seat of feeling—(心 xin), originally a picture of the aorta. Thus Chinese philosophers never drew the sharp Manichean split between the cognitive and the affective. One or the other may dominate in any particular situation, but both are active at all times in responding to and reflecting on one's environment.

Perhaps another entry into what our differences might be can come from a statement Smith made in response to a question from the audience during the course of the evening of the original lecture, a statement which certainly arched a number of eyebrows among his listeners: "Interfaith dialogue is a big thing today and I get asked about this a lot. And my answer is rather surprising to many: I am not against it. If you want to do it, go right ahead; but I am not much interested."[23]

To my mind, interfaith dialogue is absolutely necessary if the world is to become less murderous than it is at present. Some moral authority must come forward on behalf of the murdered, and religious leaders are one group that might claim that authority.

---

[23] From the transcript made by Dr. Martin Verhoeven of the tape made on the occasion of the original lecture.

But such will not be conducive to a more peaceful world unless those religious leaders speak with a single voice about peace—and about justice as well. For myself, this is what interfaith dialogue should be about. It should focus on what the world's religions have in common (as in Smith's fourteen points, and in my concept of "spiritual disciplines"), rather than on what separates them (their metaphysics, theologies, specific practices, and so forth). Not only are the metaphysical pronouncements of the world's religions incompatible with each other, they are all, as I argued earlier, incompatible with several of the pronouncements of (at least) physics, biology, and geology. Thus any interfaith dialogue about cosmology, cosmogony, ontology, or theology would be, to my mind, fruitless at best, destructive of mutual understanding at worst. It would very probably be highly salutary for dialogue if religious leaders of all faiths came to agree that the ontology reflected in Smith's diagram was the correct one, but I have no hope such will be forthcoming.

Thus, while I want much more interfaith dialogue, I want it centered on attempting to establish a rank ordering of values held by the adherents of each tradition, but currently ordered differently among them.[24] Now if Smith is not interested in interfaith

---

[24] On the difference between changing values and reordering them, see my "Two Loci of Authority," in *Confucian Cultures of Authority*, edited by Peter Hershock and Roger T. Ames (Albany: SUNY Press, 2006).

dialogue because of a reluctance to engage in meta-physics, as not seeing such dialogues as spiritually fruitful, then I, too, am not interested in interfaith dialogue. At the same time, I would hope he would be as concerned for interfaith dialogues at the moral and political level as I am.

In summary, I am strongly inclined to support Smith's overall employment of Chomsky's conceptual orientation as a means of deepening our understanding of religion, and do so for reasons that are even deeper with respect to that orientation than Huston intimates in his lecture. But Smith seems to go farther, and with his ontological pronouncements enters what I would take to be the field of theology, where I do not feel qualified to follow him.

3

THE CONVERSATION

HENRY ROSEMONT, JR., AND
HUSTON SMITH

This chapter has the appearance of a transcript of a conversation between Huston Smith and myself, and in many respects that is what it is. We met for two hours in his living room on a Monday in November, 2006, with Dr. Martin Verhoeven and the Reverend Heng Sure in attendance, the latter taping the discussion. But the present text differs from the original in several respects. First, pleasantries of the day, gross infelicities of expression, and comments on issues distant from the subject of the Universal Grammar of religion have been excised. And a number of my contributions to the discussion have been significantly abbreviated because Huston insisted that I should have the last word in our exchanges, so I have placed a number of my remarks in the chapter to follow, letting Huston be the focus of this one. I have also added some materials from the evening of the original lecture—namely, some questions from the audience, for which Huston's answers seem more appropriately placed here than earlier—and a few brief remarks made in a more informal luncheon conversation we had with Martin Verhoeven on the previous Friday.—H.R.

HR: It is very good of you to offer so much time for further discussion on the topic of a Universal Grammar of religion, to finish up what we began at your lecture (and long before that), to celebrate what we agree upon and attend to our differences. I am especially pleased that you can engage in this conversation today, as you've just recently returned from a busy weekend being honored by the Esalen Institute[1] I am also pleased that you wish to continue this conversation for the same reason I do, namely, in the hope of making a small contribution to stemming an increasing tide of hostility to religion, a hostility not at all unjustified owing to the fanaticism that accompanies many fundamentalist orientations in several faith traditions today, not to speak of the horrors perpetrated in the past by various peoples in the name of their religions.[2]

HS: That's right. And I know we also share an antipathy to most forms of relativism that are intellectually fashionable today as well. I'll follow your lead in responding to comments and questions, but I

---

[1] A video of the event is available from Phil Cousineau Events: pilgrimage@earthlink.net.

[2] Here I had intended to make reference especially to Richard Dawkins's *The God Delusion*, with some critical remarks thereon, but Professor Michelle Switzer has called my attention to a review essay of the book which has done the job much better than I could have done. It is "Lunging, Flailing, and Mispunching," by Terry Eagleton; it appeared in the *London Review of Books* 28, 19 October 2006.

do want you to have the last word on this matter, I want you to write out the final statement.

HR: Okay, if that's the way you want to do it. Let's begin with the genesis of your lecture theme of a "Universal Grammar" of religion. You were a colleague of Noam Chomsky's at MIT from the late 1950s until the early 1970s, and you surely had some knowledge of the exciting ideas that were coming out of the department of linguistics, even though you were in the philosophy department. Yet to the best of my knowledge, your Master Hsüan Hua lecture last year was the first time you attempted to integrate Chomsky's concept of Universal Grammar into your own work. Why the lengthy delay?

HS: Well, there are two reasons, both of them a little embarrassing to state, but it's all right to tape them, and keep them there. First, in the early days of the "Chomskyan Revolution," I had a general idea of his theory of a specific cognitive capacity for language acquisition, but I didn't understand fully the implications of the theory, either for language study itself, or for the applicability of the theory to other mental domains. Second, I have a passable mind, but it's not a fast mind. I don't believe, however, that the speed of a mind has anything to do with its quality. When my brothers and I were growing up in China, they seemed to understand everything the first time around. They got it. When my parents delivered me to boarding school, they told me later, their last words to the teachers were, "Don't give up on Huston. He can get it. It just takes him longer." Thus it was the janitor and I who closed things up at the end of the day. And that has been true all along. The relevance of Noam's theory to my work just didn't click for a very long time, and only really clicked when I was invited to give the Memorial Lecture.

HR: Is it more the inborn nature of much of what we have come to call—somewhat misleadingly— "knowledge of language"[3] that led you to the relevance of his theories to yours, or is it more his equally unusual (at least to many traditional philosophers of science) ideas about the proper way to conduct scientific investigations?[4]

HS: It was the former. I spun off from that and began to think that if there is a deep grammar which is hardwired into our brain, and then maybe we are hardwired in a similar way for religion. I believe that now, and since I'm also a believer in revelation, I will continue to discuss it in the Christian terms of my

---

[3] For the distinction between having knowledge of one's language and the ability to use language, see, for example, Chomsky's "Language and Interpretation: Philosophical Reflections and Empirical Inquiry," in *New Horizons in the Study of Language and Mind*.

[4] Which Chomsky calls the "Galilean style." See for example, Chomsky, *Rules and Representations*, 5ff.

upbringing. But I think the idiom can be suitably changed to accommodate other religions. God would reveal himself in the truth in the hardwiring of our minds. I believe that.

HR: Good enough, but that brings up a related question: In your lecture you used the expression "a Universal Grammar of *religion*," and you do the same on occasion in the work you were engaged in writing at the same time,[5] but elsewhere in that work in you referred to "a Universal Grammar of *worldview*"; is the shift of words significant?

HS: All religions and theologies are set within a worldview, because we need the most wide-angle lens we can have in our efforts to understand our lives religiously. Without such a lens, if a little wicked "fact" came in from left field we'd be stopped, or at least slowed down. Things have to be set within a worldview. In general, theologies just content themselves with the texts that are revealed, such as the Bible, the Qur'an, and so forth. But the truth is, if those religions are not seen with the widest angled lens possible, one cannot fully believe in them because they might be shattered by some wicked little fact.

HR: That's an appropriate response; I see now how you believe the two are linked. Here's an analogous

---

[5] Published as Huston Smith, *The Soul of Christianity* (San Francisco: Harper, 2005). See especially pp. 33ff.

question: At times—in your most ecumenical mode,
I assume—you speak of all religions. You did so
just now, and it was a part of the sixth point of your
lecture: what Christians call "God" can also be called
the "Almighty," the "Infinite," the "One," the "Real," or
other similar terms. But at other times you speak of
"revealed" religions only,[6] as you just did now; why do
you add the modifier some but not all of the time?

HS: Good question. Religion covers a multitude of
sins and a very wide territory, and I do not at all times
want to appear to be speaking for all of them. The
Mormons are a classic case. A bishop in the Mormon
Church and his wife are very good friends of mine, but
as you surely know, Mormons have a very peculiar
view of American history, and I do not want to appear
to be speaking for them. That's why the qualifier comes
in at times.

HR: While on the subject of revelation, let me
raise again a question that was asked at the lecture by
a member of the audience. If, as you stress in your
ninth point, human beings need revelation in order to
comprehend the Infinite—if God must reveal himself
to us—then, to quote the question precisely, "What
role does free will play in the attainment of sacred
knowledge when it is an individual's task to attain this
knowledge, but it seems contingent upon this Infinite

---

[6] Ibid.

power's decision whether or not to bestow it upon us?"[7] Put another way, doesn't your claim imply that if God doesn't see fit to reveal things to us, it is a waste of time for us to seek the truth on our own?

HS: Well, free will is very important, and it is a part of the goodness of creation, because if we were not given free will, we would be robots, or puppets, and would lose our dignity. Our dignity derives from our freedom, including the freedom to take an interest in religion or not. And therefore free will is very important and a part of our makeup.

HR: If you can recall the moment, the questioner was not altogether sure you had fully responded to the thrust of the question he asked, and I then jumped in, saying something like, "The spiritual disciplines that I see in every sacred tradition as embodied in their sacred texts provide a multiplicity of ways to achieve ego-reduction, which is necessary, to put it in Huston's terms, for the infinite to come in. By following these practices and disciplines—which can be found in every tradition of which I am aware—you would be open to that epiphany, to that religious experience, but it is not guaranteed that it will come. It is a gift of the spirit, so to speak. You should be optimistic that you can attain sacred knowledge if you work at it, because it is an

---

[7] From the transcript of the videotape of the evening by Jon Monday, in the library of the Institute for World Religions.

inbuilt capability, amply evidenced by numerous practitioners of every religious tradition. In this sense, too, it is like language: we have an inbuilt capacity to acquire it, and all normal people do, but not everyone attains the level of the gifted novelist, playwright, or poet; such is a gift of the spirit."[8] When I gave that response you were nodding your head next to me vigorously, which I took to be agreement with my response to the question. Is that correct?

HS: Yes, I thought you said it very well.

HR: Thanks. Let me return again now to the lecture proper. I was a bit surprised when you said in your lecture—in your fourth point—that all religions have a top-down orientation. I have never thought of Buddhism in that way, and I am pretty sure the two Buddhists here with us don't think of it that way either [Both Heng Sure and Marty Verhoeven nod their assent]. Moreover, the generalization does not, in my opinion, describe Confucianism—especially early Confucianism—at all.

HS: I place the Buddha on the same level as I place Christ. We know the story of the Buddha leaving his palace, treading several spiritual paths that were unsatisfying, until he began to sit beneath the *bo* tree, vowing not to rise until he realized the truth. And we all know the story of the awakening after forty-nine

---

[8] Ibid.

days in meditation, how the truth came to him, described metaphorically. Now I don't know whether it's legal for me to question my questioner, but where do you suppose that truth came from? To answer my own question, I think it was an insight that came that night as the morning star was twinkling, up vertical as always, the symbol for the better. To my mind, this is an exact parallel to when Jesus came out of the Jordan and heard a voice from heaven, "Thou art my son, my only begotten son."

HR: A most interesting response, which we'll all have to think about, Buddhists and non-Buddhists alike. How about Confucianism?

HS: Look who I'm being asked to lecture to on Confucianism. But where did Confucius get his wisdom, which made him the preeminent teacher in China? Correct me if I'm wrong, but isn't there a passage in the *Analects* where he is discouraged that he has never been recognized for high office? It seemed like a note of despair.

HR: There are several passages with a lament of that kind, including a few in which he seems to believe that *tian* 天—usually translated misleadingly as "Heaven"—had forsaken him,[9] and still others where

---

[9] *Analects* 11.9, for example, reads "When Yan Hui died, the Master cried, 'Oh, my! *Tian* is the ruin of me! *Tian* is the ruin of me!" Here and in the following, all Confucian quotations are from

he seemed to think *tian* had given him the task of righting the wrongs of the day by returning to the ways of the ancient sage kings[10]—all of which would strengthen your case. And a number of interpreters of Confucianism have read him as you are doing, from Matteo Ricci through Leibniz[11] down to the present day. But there's a catch. Most of these interpreters have been, like yourself, Christians with open minds and an ecumenical bent. I certainly agree that throughout the *Analects* it is fairly clear that Confucius believed he had a mission. But I and several other commentators on the text today would answer your question differently.[12] In the first place, Confucius at times denies he has any knowledge or wisdom (9.8), or a little at best (7.28); and that his learning came from other people: "In strolling in the company of just two other persons, I am bound to find a teacher. Identifying their strengths, I follow them, and identifying their weaknesses, I reform myself accordingly" (7.22). Or

---

The Analects of Confucius: A Philosophical Translation, translated by Roger T. Ames and Henry Rosemont, Jr. (New York: Random House/ Ballantine Books, 1998). Hereafter cited by chapter and section.

[10] *Analects* 9.5.

[11] For details, see *Leibniz: Writings on China,* translated and edited by Daniel J. Cook and Henry Rosemont, Jr. (Chicago: Open Court, 1994).

[12] To name just two: Herbert Fingarette, most especially in his classic *Confucius: The Secular as Sacred* (New York: Harper and Row, 1972), and *Thinking Through Confucius* by David L. Hall and Roger T. Ames (Albany, NY: SUNY Press, 1987).

again: "I find inspiration by intoning the *Songs*, I learn where to stand from observing ritual propriety [*li*], and I find fulfillment in playing music" (8.8). For myself, I don't believe these and similar passages are simply expressions of modesty, for at other times the Master was straightforward in describing his virtues. All of this, to me, takes place within a single plane of existence, the worldly; or at the least, that he can be understood and explained in that way. I fear that on this count we can only agree to disagree.

HS: Well, perhaps. You see, a number of people have said that Huston Smith has this optical defect: He sees similarities everywhere. It's rather true. It's my way of stressing the parity of all of the major religions that have shaped civilization. But there's more. Hear this: This ground on which I stand is the Promised Land, and this body is the body of the Buddha. What we have to understand is that the spirit, or whatever word you would like to use in its stead, knows nothing of geography. This is why I believe Bell's Theorem is as significant for religion as it is for physics, and it has thus far been borne out experimentally. Up, down, right, left, we live in a nonlocal universe, wherein the interconnectedness of all things, not their discreteness, is what is important.[13]

---

[13] For a fairly nontechnical account of the potential significance of Bell's Theorem for religion, see Robert Gilman, "The Next Great Turning," *Context* (Winter 1993).

HR: I don't recall reading about what you see as the spiritual significance of Bell's Theorem in any of your writings. Is this another recent meditation?

HS: Well, I've written a lot, and much of it lately. I think, if I've taken up the topic, it would be in either *Why Religion Matters* or *The Way Things Are*.[14]

HR: Let me now range a bit more broadly if I may, so that we can view your notion of a Universal Grammar of religion in living context—your own.

HS: By all means. I'm not tired at all.

HR: Although you have traveled the world over studying and practicing almost all of the world's religions, you have always remained with Christian Protestantism in general, and Methodism in particular, as your faith tradition. Can you say why?

HS: A friend who knows me very well said, "Huston, you know full well that the only thing that keeps you in that wishy-washy Methodist church is ancestor worship and filial piety." As I said, this friend knows me very well indeed. That is the tradition I was steeped in. If I may quote His Holiness the Dalai

---

[14] Huston Smith, *Why Religion Matters* (Harper: San Francisco, 2000), and Huston Smith and Phil Cousineau, *The Way Things Are* (Berkeley: University of California Press, 2005).

Lama, he replied when he was asked about conversion, "Well, it's best if you can stay in the heritage that raised you because your impulses are just attuned thereto." I thought to myself, "Silent Night" touches me, but I can't expect it to touch a Confucian the way it touches me. Then His Holiness went on to say that if you have been bruised by your own tradition, then you should look around. I was not bruised.

HR: Paradoxically—though perhaps not to someone born and raised in China—that is a very Confucian justification for your Methodist beliefs and practices, considering that ancestor worship and filial piety are cornerstones of the Confucian secular temple.

HS: Well, once in a while I gaze into the truth.

HR: Other than Christianity, is there one of the other faith traditions that has had more of an impact on your life than the others?

HS: I will give you a straightforward answer to that question, but must preface it by saying that I hope I die before anything would budge me from my conviction of the parity of the eight traditions that have shaped civilizations, as I've already said earlier. But each person latches on to one of the eight for historical reasons—I mean historical in the personal sense— and in my personal history Islam, especially the Sufi tradition, has had the greatest impact on me next to

Christianity. This happened because I stumbled upon a savant (as I tend to speak of him), Frithjof Schuon, who solved a paradox that I had been unable to solve myself, namely, believing in the parity of the eight traditions on the one hand, and believing in unity on the other.

HR: His thesis is stated succinctly in the title of his best-known work, *The Transcendent Unity of Religions,* which you have cited many times. I have used that work several times in philosophy of religion classes over the years, with good effect, even though it is not at all an easy book to read. Your lengthy preface to the work helped orient a lot of readers to what was to come.[15]

HS: Yes, Harper's said they would bring out an English edition to the book if I would write a preface for it, so I did. Schuon had solved my dilemma with a single stroke. Religions are like trousers—have I told you this joke before?—singular at the top and plural at the bottom. I love that. And he introduced the words "esoteric" and "exoteric" into the comparative study of religion in a new way. On the exoteric side, the explicit philosophies and theologies of the eight traditions are different. But esoterically—as in my fourteen points and in my diagram—religions are one, like the kernel inside the walnut.

---

[15] Frithjof Schuon, *The Transcendent Unity of Religions* (New York: Harper & Row, 1975).

HR: I'm a little surprised that you feel the closest to the Sufi tradition of Islamic mysticism when the mystical tradition has not occupied a prominent place in the history of Christianity. Yes, we have Meister Eckhart, San Juan de la Cruz, Teresa of Avila, and a few others, but in general mysticism plays only a minor role in the Christian heritage, especially when compared to the Sufi—or the Hindu, Buddhist, and Daoist traditions, not to mention the Cabbalists.

HS: Well, St. Augustine, who shaped the mind of Europe for over a millennium, said, "Thou hast made us for thyself and our hearts are restless till they find themselves in Thee." What more do we need?

HR: Perhaps we needed an Augustine who could say that without feeling guilty about snitching a few apples. But to pursue this point would take us rather far afield. Let me turn now instead to two questions that came from the audience at your lecture, your brief answers to which caused them all to sit bolt upright in the pews. Perhaps by addressing them now we can get another angle on the "Universal Grammar of religion." The first question was how you saw your fourteen points contributing to interfaith dialogue, and you replied that you had no interest in interfaith dialogue, although it was fine if anyone else wanted to do it. Because there were many more questioners waiting to be heard, you didn't have time to give a full reply, but perhaps you can do so now: Why don't you care about interfaith dialogue?

HS: First, let me say that the interfaith dialogue you and the questioner are referring to does not need my fourteen points. But we are in a new time. With globalization, the religions of the world are rubbing shoulders with each other as never before, and for those genuinely interested in the life of the spirit, this poses a problem that is going to be with us for decades, maybe even centuries. Namely, how do we combine depth in our own faith with openness to others? There is no formula for that. We each have to work it out in our own way. But to address the query more directly, it is true that people are often thrown when I say that I am not interested in interfaith dialogue, especially since I have spent so much of my life studying and practicing the several faith traditions, as you were so generous in pointing up in your response to the lecture, Henry.

But let me elaborate. I did my homework on those eight religions in the library, read the best books I could find, and then followed up by wanting to personalize my studies and seeking out the most profound exponents of each tradition that I could get wind of. Suzuki Daisetz was one—as I remember, Henry, you wrote your dissertation on him—he was one, and I made pilgrimages apprenticing myself to him and to others, and even plunged myself into their practices, but I never went to dialogue. If any of these exponents had asked me a question about Christianity or philosophy, of course I would have answered.

But with the exception of his Holiness the Dalai Lama, no one ever did, and I believe he did largely because he is a world figure, and he needs to ask such questions. I had the honor of hosting him on his first visit to the United States. He said that one of the things he wanted to do was spend three days at the Harvard Divinity School. "Not to give a lecture," he said, "but to learn from them." But none of the other teachers I visited were interested in dialogue at all. Let me conclude by emphasizing again that if you want to do that, feel free. I didn't say I was against it. I just don't care about it.

HR: I myself am disinclined to interfaith dialogues if they are just about metaphysics and theologies, which I see as doing more harm than good. Cross-cultural understanding that is supposed to accompany interfaith dialogue is achieved at the level of ethics and specific spiritual disciplines and rituals, that is, dialogues about real-world *practices.* I'll want to return to this point in my closing remarks, but let me turn now to the other unexpected answer you gave to a question from the audience. The question was, "What selectional advantage might a Universal Grammar of religion have conferred on our species?" You replied by expressing a general unhappiness with such types of question—but did so most graciously—and I am confident Chomsky would share your uneasiness, as I explained in my revised response.

Given that I know you are no more impressed with the notion of intelligent design than I—or any other person without a hidden agenda—have ever been, how do you describe your objection to such questions?

HS: Let me briefly state my view of the matter. No amount of talk of selectional advantage will ever begin to explain how we get to what the scholastics called the *imago dei*, the image of God, the spark of the divine, which all the religions believe is the essence of the human self, and that this essence comes from else-where than survival of the fittest or any other purely evolutionary concept. But to say this is to take religion very seriously, which the intellectual journals and magazines do not want to do. Religion has been hijacked by politics, and no one wants to say anything supportive of religion in any other than a secularist fashion. I think this is a weathervane of where we are today, as you so nicely put it at the beginning of our session.

HR: I'm confident that Chomsky would agree that asking for the survival function of every trait of every organism is very bad science. And I believe he would concur with me that it is worse than that, for in one sense, any attempt at wholesale reductionism can all too easily lead to efforts by some people—the "experts" and the powerful who employ them—to control other people, the great majority of ordinary human beings. Behaviorism was only the most blatant of such so-called scientific efforts.[16] Some practitioners of reductionism surely have no authoritarian tendencies, but given how unfruitful scientifically so much of this work has been for so long, one must wonder about why it endures so steadfastly. With regard to religion, you've already hinted that the answer lies in the current antipathy to religion, caused as much by a certain intellectual arrogance as by the horrors that religious fanatics are visiting on one another today.

Mentioning Chomsky again gives us the opportunity to return to the topic of the Universal Grammar of religion. According to my reading of Chomsky, environmental stimuli do not *shape* our responses in areas for which we have an innate mental capacity, they *trigger* the responses. With the language capacity, for example, it must be triggered by hearing human language. The "wild boy" of Aveyon might have understood a bit of what wolves signaled with their growls, howls, and other behaviors, but he didn't learn "wolf language" except metaphorically (and misleadingly). He didn't learn language at all.[17]

---

[16] A not uncommon theme in much of Chomsky's writing, especially those in the interstices between his linguistics and his political work, such as "Psychology and Ideology" in *For Reasons of State*.

[17] The first study made of a feral child, made in the early nineteenth century by J. M.G. Itard. See *The Wild Boy of Aveyon*,

The case is the same with the other specific cognitive capacities that Chomsky postulates for the human mind: facial recognition, personality discrimination, music, and so forth. Unless we see faces, we obviously won't be able to exercise our capacity to recognize them. We need only a minimal number of environmental inputs for the capacity to begin working, but we do need some to *trigger* the capacity.[18] If I am right on this count, what bearing does it have on your use of his expression "Universal Grammar" for religion?

HS: Let me be sure I understand you, and Chomsky, correctly. In the last lecture I heard him give, if I remember it correctly, he said different species had different innate capacities, and I surely agree. Construction people would give their eyeteeth for the knack ants have for building anthills. All the ants seem to know what the others are doing and what their own jobs are. And those engineers would also probably give their eyeteeth to be able to build bird's nests with only a scrap of this and a scrap of that, and a little saliva, yet have a sturdy home as a the result. Now what are we humans good at? As I believe Chomsky said, we have a capacity for language, and a capacity for science, among others. No other species has those two capacities.

---

translated by G. Humphrey and M. Humphrey (New York: Appleton-Century-Crofts, 1962).

[18] For more on shaping and triggering stimuli, see Rosemont, "Against Relativism."

And I believe we have a third, a capacity for the divine.

HR: You are right that Chomsky maintains that we have a science-forming capacity, but it is different than the language capacity in some crucial respects, especially in his insistence, first, that there are a number of possible sciences inaccessible to human beings, mentally and physiologically constituted as they are, and secondly, we can certainly learn physics, but watching apples fall from a tree does not "trigger" any knowledge of physics on its own. Unlike the grammar of one's native language, physics must be consciously taught and studied.[19] But now let me ask you to expand your answer: Do you believe some "spark of the divine" triggers this religious orientation in us?

HS: Yes, I think I covered this in saying that we are hard-wired in our minds for the divine.

HR: Let me press you a bit. If the distinction I make between shaping and triggering is warranted, don't we need some kind of trigger for the divine to come to us, so to speak?

HS: You're pressing me, good friend, but that is what philosophers are supposed to do to each other,

---

[19] For discussion of both he science-forming capacity, and its limits, see, for example, Chomsky, *Rules and Representations*, 250ff.

isn't it? Let me respond by recalling an exchange I had with the well-known Christian philosopher Alvin Plantinga. Once, when asked what proof he could offer for the existence of God, I believe he answered, "How can I look for a proof of God's existence when God's existence is more evident to me than anything else that I might argue from?" and I think of that as answering your question. The evidence is the whole universe around us.

HR: That is certainly a significant answer, but like Plantinga's it is a showstopper, and you're departing somewhat from the Chomskyan model, or so it seems to me. Again, in his view, hearing human language triggers specifiable responses in all normal human beings, largely independently of their intelligence and motivation. But it seems that with religion, to get that sense of the self-evidence of God, or, more neutrally, the divine, you need a discipline. Admittedly, some people may have life-transforming epiphanies, seemingly spontaneously,[20] but such persons are rare. For the most part, apprehending the divine, achieving a sense of belonging, requires a spiritual discipline of

---

[20] For myself, one striking example was the case of Arthur Koestler, who had a mystical experience while imprisoned by the Falangists during the Spanish Civil War, while attempting to recall Euclid's proof that there is no greatest prime in his effort to take his mind away from thinking about the likelihood that he was going to be executed shortly. See A. Koestler, *The Invisible Writing* (New York: Macmillan, 1954), especially chap. 4.

one kind or another—of which all religions provide several. It will not simply come to you. There are a lot of people who have no sense of divinity whatsoever, however it may be defined; they have no religious impulse at all. This will not happen with language, facial recognition, and so forth. Isn't there a difference here that we cannot overlook?

HS: You are putting the cart before the horse. In a word, the natural impulse is piety. I agree that to deepen the sense of piety requires discipline. Wonder might help explain what I mean: our childlike wonder that there is a world at all.

HR: Wouldn't it be healthy for the whole world if that sense of wonder could be recaptured? Unfortunately, the cart has a motor today, and people drive their carts too rapidly for the scenery speeding by to inspire a sense of wonder and consequent piety. And just as unfortunately, more personally, I see that we have no more time. This has been a most productive discussion, good sir, at least from my perspective. I hope it was neither too taxing nor irrelevant for you. Thanks so much.

HS: I'm the one to thank you. Henry, may my remarks help in the production of a useful little volume, the last words of which I'm happy to put in your hands.

4

THE SUMMATION

HENRY ROSEMONT, JR.

In this closing essay I attempt to weave together the several strands of our dialogue, both to aid the reader in seeing where Huston Smith and I are in agreement on the issues despite our differing visions of the nature of religion, and where we are not. While technically this is the "last word" on the issues, it is only so for this little book. I will continue to think about them, and suspect he will too; our aim, in significant measure, has been to get the reader to continue thinking about them as well.

To the reader of this book—or of almost any of Huston Smith's writings—it should be clear that he has a vision of religion, and that it is reflected in the cosmos and in human beings. He has claimed, too, in this regard, that such visions are more compelling than arguments (as we saw in the introduction).[1] Hence it would seem that two people with very differing visions would each be incapable of persuading the other of the mistaken character of any beliefs central to the other's vision, no matter how clear and incontrovertible the

---

[1] See p. xvi and note 3.

facts adduced, or how valid the logical relations made manifest between them.

Consequently this concluding chapter is not intended to refute any of Huston Smith's claims. My own position, as will become clear, precludes any efforts at such refutation, and he, I believe, would say of mine not that it is mistaken, but that it is incomplete. Therefore it seems best for me to simply juxtapose our visions clearly enough so that the reader may place their similarities and differences in perspective and compare them to the reader's own position. My aim in proceeding in this way is thus to help other students of religion to more clearly focus their own visions thereof, understand the presuppositions of their visions, and reevaluate opposing visions with greater sympathy.

I will begin by first outlining the many areas in the study and practice of religion where I believe Huston and I are in agreement on the issues—or, as he might want to put it, where our visions have significant overlap. I will then go on to put forth and attempt to justify those aspects of my overall view that seem to me to be incommensurable with his. With one exception, our greatest areas of overlap are exactly those where we also diverge substantively: in our views of human nature, as described by the "Universal Grammar"; relatedly, in our belief in the importance of religion for human flourishing; and, relatedly again, in our views on evolution; and finally, in our belief in the parity of the world's spiritual traditions. The exception is in the field of ontology: His is luxuriant and full, mine is fairly austere. I will take up each of these issues in turn.

Chomsky's theory of the modular nature of the human mind is the one that seems to me to most accurately fit the preponderance not only of scientific research in the human sciences—anthropology and psychology no less than linguistics—but of commonsense folklore as well. We are not surprised when a five-year-old recognizes his Uncle John and immediately distinguishes him from his Uncle Harry, even if the child hasn't seen either of them more than a time or two in the past year. But we would be surprised indeed if the child also recognized that Uncle John was driving a 2002 Toyota Camry rather than his similarly colored 2004 Ford, and the surprise would turn to astonishment if we were told the child has not received any explicit instruction in automobile recognition. Why is this so? Or, although at times we make serious mistakes, why are we able to develop a pretty good idea of a new acquaintance's personality after just a few meetings? And why did we not imitate the frequent grammatical lapses we encountered daily when we were young?[2]

Huston Smith and I are of a piece on this score. Accepting Chomsky's position as I do, "Plato's problem" becomes insoluble if it is presumed that the human mind is like the blank slate or *tabula rasa* of

---

[2] Rosemont, "Against Relativism," has additional arguments on these points. And cf. n. 4 below.

Enlightenment-era British empiricism, or twentieth-century behaviorism of a Skinnerian sort. Rather must we posit innate mechanisms in the human mind, specify their properties, and then test them as best we can, modifying our hypotheses about them in the face of counterevidence that cannot be otherwise explained. This methodology was scorned for the greater part of the twentieth century, and its resurgence in the last few decades is in no small measure due to Chomsky's work.[3] That is, positing innate mechanisms to account for highly sophisticated human responses to a minimum of environmental stimuli is not at all like saying that things fall because they have a downward tendency.[4] In the case of a propensity for religious behavior, the strongest evidence for its being innate is simply its ubiquity. There do not seem to be any cultures, past or present, that have not had religion as central to their art, music, moral norms, social structure, and much more, no matter what their

---

[3] Chomsky has identified his approach to the study of language as a return to the insights of the Port-Royal grammarians, Descartes and von Humboldt, a return he labeled a "rationalist" rather than the "empiricist" methodology common in linguistics at least since the time of Leonard Bloomfield's *Language* (New York: Holt, Rinehart & Winston, 1933). Chomsky discusses his intellectual forebears in *Cartesian Linguistics* (New York: Harper & Row, 1966).

[4] See my "Gathering Evidence for Linguistic Innateness," *Synthese* 38 (May 1978) for further argument on this score. See n. 2 here as well.

environmental circumstances. Smith's diagram is thus in at least one sense to be read as an "argument" on behalf of a Universal Grammar of religion.

Relatedly, religion has led to levels of human flourishing the world over, past and present. "Not by bread alone" seems to have paraphrases in virtually every culture (certainly in China, India, and ancient Greece no less than in the Judaic-Christian traditions). Religion has inspired the search for knowledge, compassion, courage, fortitude, selflessness, and, in general, almost all of the excellences that have been highly valued cross-culturally. Smith is at least as sensitive as I am to the manifold horrors that have been perpetrated in the name of religion as well, but to follow those atheists and agnostics who would rid the world of it is far too draconian a measure (and it would be an altogether unsuccessful enterprise anyway).[5] Clearly I share the view of the negative writers that the metaphysical and theological pronouncements of the world's religions—the focus tends to be on the Abrahamic faiths—cannot be made to square with the findings of science, and science must win these disputes for all rational people. But before rejecting the world's religions altogether, we should reflect for a moment on their highest heroes and heroines, they are overwhelmingly healers and peacemakers. From St. Francis to Gandhi, Al-Ghazali to the Buddha, Black

---

[5] This point is taken from my *Rationality and Religious Experience*.

Elk to Guan Yin, it is compassion that we see, and a hunger for peace, not anger or a thirst for vengeance.

Smith and I also agree that the contribution religion makes to human flourishing—and solidarity as well—is not to be seen solely, or even primarily, as adaptive, and I at least am confident that Chomsky would join us in our overall argument on this score.[6] Moreover, it is hard for me to see the relevance of Darwin on this point, and I believe that explains at least partially why Smith dealt so briefly with the question both after his lecture and during our conversation. Learning that our religious impulses may have been evolutionarily helpful would very probably not affect those impulses at all. It may well be, for example, highly adaptive for me to believe without question that my family members care deeply about me, but the fact of adaptation—tribal cohesiveness and all that, if it is indeed a fact—diminishes my belief that my family members care deeply about me not one whit, and I do not believe I am at all unusual in this regard.

Perhaps most important of all, Huston Smith and I believe that the similarities among and between the world's religions far outweigh their differences in importance. The latter are by no means inconsequential: millions of people have slaughtered and been slaughtered over the centuries fighting over whose God

---

[6] See the quote from him in chap. 2, n. 2.

should reign supreme, and/or how He was properly to be worshipped—a nauseous history that continues to this day. These differences, however, are largely found in the areas of cosmology, myths, and legends, and specific rituals linked thereto. But, for both of us, the sacred texts become strikingly similar if we look to them for spiritual guidance. For myself all sacred texts outline a multiplicity of spiritual disciplines in order to achieve religious experiences here and now. Smith, on the other hand, seeks their ontological foundations. But to keep to a distinction made early on by Chomsky in developing his generative grammar, both Smith and I are in agreement that at a deep level, the similarities among all the world's religions are far more significant than the differences that are manifest on their surface.[7]

A number of people still find this view highly implausible, for a number of reasons, not least being the horrors practitioners of one faith, or sect therein, have visited on others, as just mentioned. Another reason is that it is not easy to read the cosmologies figuratively; Siva the Destroyer's *lingam* rising from the ocean deep is a very different image of human creation than God the Master Surgeon anesthetizing Adam

------

[7] Although Chomsky himself used the terms "deep structure" and "surface structure" to describe the syntactic patterns of sentences in his early writings, he later referred to those patterns as "D-structures" and S-structures" respectively, for reasons that are too narrowly a matter of linguistics to warrant describing herein. See Chomsky, *Rules and Representations,* 145, for the usage of the new terms, and their links to the old.

before removing a part of his thoracic cavity to secure a companion for him.

But the most important reason, I believe, for the reluctance of so many people to appreciate the parity of the world's religion is simply that a belief in a single Supreme Being, God, continues to be equated with religion now no less than when the formal study of religion began in the West almost five centuries ago. If there is no Supreme Being (as in Buddhism and Confucianism), how could there be religion? If there are a multiplicity of Gods (as in Hinduism and Daoism), how could there be religion?[8]

To be sure, Huston Smith's *The World's Religions,* in all of its incarnations, has done a great deal to dispel the idea of equating religion with belief in a personal God, and the more tolerant behavior toward practitioners of other faiths that we see every day now is significantly attributable to that book. But much more remains to be done, and in my opinion will best be done by attending much less to *beliefs* (cosmologies, myths, legends), and much more to *practices* (rituals, prayer, moral acts, worship). When studying the "other" on this score, we should check the temptation

---

[8] For an unusual but incisive discussion of the points advanced in this paragraph and the preceding one, see S. N. Balagangadhara, *'The Heathen in his Blindness'* . . . : *Asia, The West, and the Dynamic of Religion* (Leiden: E.J. Brill, 1994), and my critique thereof, "How Do You Learn to be Religious?" in *Cultural Dynamics* 8, no. 2 (July 1996).

to begin with "What do they believe?" and instead ask "What do they do?"

In brief compass, then, these are the areas in which Huston Smith and I are as one.

To segue into where we differ in these same areas I will first take up briefly the single issue on which we are farthest apart: ontological commitments. I should like to say that I make none and that he makes many in our approaches to religion and its study, but I know that can't be so; it is hard to say anything at all, let alone when philosophy or theology are being discussed, without presupposing that there are certain things in the universe.

More modestly then, my vision of religion suggests that I not proffer a specific view of the universe; that I make as few ontological commitments as possible when discussing either religion or the universe; and that I not enter into quarrels with those who make explicit ontological claims. Huston Smith's vision, on the other hand obliges him to make some strong commitments to a specific picture of the universe, and hence to a rich ontology as well. As he says explicitly, "I do not see how it is possible to deal philosophically with spiritual matters without a hierarchical ontology."[9]

That ontology is graphically depicted in Smith's diagram: levels of reality hierarchically ordered

-----

[9] Huston Smith, "Spiritual Discipline in Zen and Comparative Perspective," in *Essays On World Religions*, edited by M. Darrol Bryant (New York: Paragon House, 1992), 111n11.

outward in height, inward in depth (notice the arrows signifying the dual gaze of the person in the center). His depiction mirrors what Aldous Huxley and others have called the "Perennial Philosophy." Huxley wrote:

> More than twenty-five centuries have passed since what has been called the Perennial Philosophy was first committed to writing; and in the course of those centuries it has found expression. . . . In Vedanta and Hebrew prophecy, in the Tao Teh King and the Platonic dialogues, in the Gospel according to St. John and Mahayana theology, in Plotinus and the Areopagite, among the Persian Sufis and the Christian mystics of the Middle Ages and the Renaissance. But . . . [it is] only in the act of contemplation, when words and even personality are transcended, that the pure state of the Perennial Philosophy can actually be known. The records left by those who have known it in this way make it abundantly clear that all of them, whether Hindu, Buddhist, Taoist, Christian or Mohammedan, were attempting to describe the same essentially indescribable fact.[10]

I can begin to communicate my uneasiness with this position by noting that Confucianism is missing from Huxley's catalogue, and even Smith does not give it a specific arc in his circle, but puts it in with "Chinese

---

[10] Aldous Huxley, introduction to the *Bhagavad-Gita*, translated by Swami Prabhavananda and Christopher Isherwood (New York: Mentor Books, 1951), 11–12.

religions." Now if their ontological orientation is correct, it must follow either that Confucianism should not be described as a religion, or that it is a strong counterexample to claims for a "Perennial Philosophy."

I have rejected the first alternative; I maintain strongly that Confucianism is a religion.[11] At the same time, I appreciate that Confucianism might not be seen as a "strong" counterexample to Huxley, Huston Smith, or other perennialists because the Confucian tradition does not include a significant meditative component in it. There is certainly mention of meditation in Neo-Confucian writings, but this was due to the influence of Buddhism, which over the course of a millennium had taken root in Chinese soil. But "Confucian mystic" sounds odd, for the tradition does not have sages of this kind akin to Meister Eckhart and Santa Teresa of Avila. Nor does Confucianism, to the best of my knowledge of the texts, accord anyone a title equivalent to "saint."

Further, I have attempted to conduct a *Gedanken-*experiment, imagining I was a Confucian scholar who, having studied the world's religions, came up with the parallels between them that Smith draws and Huxley

---

[11] In several papers, among them "Is There a Path of Spiritual Progress in the Texts of Early Confucianism?" in *Confucian Spirituality*, vol. 1, edited by Tu Weiming and Mary Evelyn Tucker (New York: Crossroad Publishing Company, 2003). The essays by Roger Ames and Deborah Sommer in the same volume are also of direct relevance on this issue.

wrote about. While I do not place a great deal of faith in my ability to think just like a classical Confucian scholar (how could I know I had it right?), I believe I would not be able to see the same ontological parallels that Huxley and Smith have seen; even though I grant that Jews, Christians, and Muslims might see them easily. Put another way: Smith's scheme seems too Abrahamic to justify the all-inclusive ontological conclusions he wants to draw from it, or for that matter to justify any purely ontological conclusions at all. To stay with my present example, classical Confucianism is not very metaphysical in orientation, or in fact.[12]

Accepting that the parallels in the sacred texts of the world's religions are there to be seen, the conclusion I draw from them is that mystical experiences, or at least the possibility of having such, are part of the answer to the question of what it is to be a human being. On this point Huston and I agree. But for him (and Huxley et al.) mystical experiences are a necessary condition for apprehending the perennial philosophy. I, however, am inclined to believe that for many religious traditions contemplative practice culminating in mystical experience is only *one* spiritual discipline among several leading to one kind of religious experience or another. Thus, that Confucianism has no strong mystical dimension does not have to be

---

[12] The texts suggest an aesthetic rather than a logical—or metaphysical—order, following David Hall and Roger Ames, *Thinking Through Confucius* (Albany, NY: SUNY Press, 1987).

surprising, even though the tradition definitely provides guidance for achieving religious experiences. Similarly, the Christian tradition—despite it several contemplative exemplars—does not emphasize mystical experiences to anywhere near the extent the Hindu and Buddhist heritages do, for example. Both Christians and Confucians emphasized different spiritual disciplines.

That is to say, my claim is that the capacity to have mystical and other religious experiences is a homoversal, a component of the "Universal Grammar" of religion with which we are all endowed. I thus reject deconstructionist and related claims that all such experiences are solely socially constructed. For myself, such experiences come about when adepts have become sufficiently skilled in meditative techniques to completely surrender the "I," the ego, for a period of time—and yet not fall asleep—and the accounts they give of these experiences will reflect their specific religious and cultural backgrounds.[13] But my own readings of the mystical texts of other traditions suggest to me that mystical experience is importantly the bridging of the divide between self and world, which Smith mentioned in his lecture, an indirect awareness of what I can only describe clumsily as un-self-consciousness; the lack of specific experiential

[13] For further argument, see the essays in Robert K. C. Foreman, *Innate Capacity: Mysticism, Psychology and Philosophy* (Oxford: Oxford University Press, 1998).

content is what allows mystics the world over—to all of whom, I am strongly inclined to attribute sincerity—to attempt to account for their experiences in images and metaphors religiously familiar to them and their audiences.[14]

Consequently, I can affirm the parity of the world's religions with Smith without concluding that their remarkable similarities justify asserting the existence of the hierarchically-ordered reality beyond the human realm they seem to describe; I am content claiming to find homoversal properties reflected in sacred texts— properties of every human being, physiologically and mentally equipped as they are.

In just the same way, I can agree with Smith that through their sacred texts, their music, rituals, disciplines, and the like, the world's religions have contributed much to human flourishing, and can contribute to even more of it when and if the more implausible, exclusivistic, absolutist, and morally questionable elements found in the sacred texts are quietly ignored, or fundamentally reinterpreted to accord with contemporary aesthetic, social, and moral sensibilities. These are, to my mind, the most pressing tasks facing theologians and textual scholars in each of the world's spiritual heritages.

---

[14] In these and related views on mysticism I have been influenced by the writings of W. T. Stace. See his *Mysticism and Philosophy* (Palgrave Macmillan, 1960), and his introduction to the work he edited, *The Teachings of the Mystics* (New York: Mentor Books, 1960).

Similarly, I can ignore the "Darwin question" as Huston Smith wishes to do, but I do so for reasons different from his. He is concerned to affirm ontologically the hierarchical reality he has found in the higher reaches of sacred writings, a reality he believes is independent of human perception. A significant part of his reason for such affirmation, again—apart from his own Christian background—is his belief, reflected clearly in his diagram, in the similarities in describing reality found in those texts—similarities which he is certain cannot be mere coincidence; adepts the world over must have seen the universe as it truly is. Whether this vision is adaptive or not in the Darwinian sense need not be of any interest to him. Presumably seeing reality as "it really is" would be adaptive, but trivial for advancing our understanding of religion and religious experience.

Put another way, Smith's view as seen in his diagram is basically answering the question "What is reality like?" by reference to the saints and sages of the world's religious heritages who have attempted to answer the same question. His justification of the hierarchical ordering exhibited in his diagram is the similar descriptions of that reality found in the world's sacred texts as he reads them, written over and across vast distances of time, space, language, and culture. If that is indeed the question he is answering, then the "Darwin question" ceases to be relevant.

But that is not the kind of question with respect to religion contemporary social scientists are asking within a Darwinian theoretical framework. That is, they are not asking a question like "Does God exist?" Or, in the present case, "Is reality hierarchically ordered?" but rather "Given that so many people, over and across vast distances of time, space, language and culture have believed in God (or a hierarchical ordering of reality), what is the survival value of such a belief?" Some of these scholars—anthropologists, psychologists—have said the belief is adaptive, and they have attempted to adduce arguments therefrom. Other scholars have said it is not adaptive, but a byproduct, like spandrels, of some other trait or belief that was adaptive. Still a third group maintains that the belief was originally adaptive, but as our minds and cultures have evolved, such a belief is no longer to be seen as adaptive.[15]

Now if this is a correct account of "the religion question" in contemporary social science, we can see more directly why Huston Smith would be indifferent to answers given to the second formulation of the question, and understand but not overly sympathize with social scientists who didn't want to ask the first.

With respect to the phenomena of all types of religious experience I, too, am indifferent to all three

---

[15] Happily for my labors in this book, an excellent overall and not overly technical account of this whole issue appeared in the *New York Times Magazine* just as I began this chapter, issue of March 7, 2007. I am very grateful to my Newport neighbor and friend Bonnie Watson for calling this article to my attention.

answers proffered for the second formulation of the question, even though the focus has shifted from the world "out there" to *Homo sapiens,* for I do not think any purported answer to the evolutionary formulation of the question contributes much to deepening our understanding of the facts of religious beliefs, and even more importantly, the facts of religious experiences. That is to say, just as I not believe I can move from accounts of how human beings do (can, must) view the world to ontological statements about the way the world "really is," so too do I not believe being told that a belief in God or a hierarchically ordered world and universe is or is not adaptive helps me understand or follow the spiritual disciplines described in sacred texts, or to experience the hierarchy. I am primarily interested in the *facts* of these similarities in belief, practices, and experiences among and between all human beings as a response to their very different environments across and over vast distances of time, space, language, and culture, for I believe these facts signal a homoversal property of human beings, physically and mentally constituted as they are.

Explaining the function(s) this shared property may serve could well be a potentially legitimate scientific endeavor. I am, however, personally skeptical of it ever being done with evidence that would outweigh speculation convincingly. And even if such did occur, I doubt that the explanation would be helpful in seeking wisdom in the sacred texts of the world's religions. Nor would it enhance our innate capacity to open ourselves more fully to the religious experiences described so frequently by practitioners the world over, past and present; experiences which assist them in living lives with full measures of peace, serenity and dignity as they encounter not only the sorrows, but the joys as well, of being human in, and attempting to improve our all-too-human world while still in that world.

In concluding, I am strongly tempted to quote Alexander Pope as an exhortation to Huston:

> Know then thyself, presume not God to scan
> The proper study of Mankind is man.[16]

But I fear he would immediately respond, "There are more things in Heaven and earth, Henry, than are dreamt of in your philosophy."[17]

---

[16] In his "Essay on Man." *Alexander Pope: Selected Poetry*, edited by Douglas Grant (London: Penguin, 1985).

[17] *Hamlet*, act 1, scene 5.

BOOKS BY
HUSTON SMITH

The Religions of Man. San Francisco: HarperCollins, 1958. Revised as *The World's Religions: Our Great Wisdom Traditions*. San Francisco: Harper San Francisco, 1991.

Forgotten Truth: The Common Vision of the World's Religions. San Francisco: Harper San Francisco, 1976.

Beyond the Postmodern Mind. Wheaton, IL: Theosophical Publishing House, 1984. 3rd ed., Quest Books, 2003.

One Nation Under God: The Triumph of the Native American Church. Santa Fe, NM: Clear Light Books, 1986.

Essays on World Religion. Edited by M. Darrol Bryant. St. Paul, MN: Paragon House, 1992.

The Illustrated World's Religions: A Guide to Our Wisdom Traditions. San Francisco: Harper San Francisco, 1995.

Cleansing the Doors of Perception: The Religious Significance of Entheogenic Plants and Chemicals. Los Angeles: Tarcher/Putnam, 2000.

Islam: A Concise Introduction. Harper San Francisco, 2001.

Why Religion Matters: The Fate of the Human Spirit in an Age of Disbelief. San Francisco: Harper San Francisco, 2001.

The Way Things Are: Conversations with Huston Smith on the Spiritual Life. Edited by Philip Cousineau. Berkeley: University of California Press, 2003.

Buddhism: A Concise Introduction. With Philip Novak. San Francisco: Harper San Francisco, 2004.

The Soul of Christianity: Restoring the Great Tradition. San Francisco: Harper San Francisco, 2005.

A Seat at the Table: Huston Smith in Conversation with Native Americans on Religious Freedom. Berkeley: University of California Press, 2006.

BOOKS BY HUSTON SMITH

BOOKS BY
HENRY ROSEMONT, JR.

A Chinese Mirror: Moral Reflections on Political Economy and Society. Chicago: Open Court, 1991. Chinese translation, 2005.

Rationality and Religious Experience: The Continuing Relevance of the World's Spiritual Traditions. Chicago: Open Court, 2001.

Radical Confucianism (forthcoming).

Books Edited

Work, Technology and Education: Dissenting Essays in the Intellectual Foundations of American Education. With Walter Feinberg. Urbana: University of Illinois Press, 1975.

Studies in Classical Chinese Thought. With Benjamin I. Schwartz. Thematic Studies series of the *Journal of the American Academy of Religion*. Scholars Press, 1979.

Explorations in Early Chinese Cosmology. Thematic Studies series of the *Journal of the American Academy of Religion*. Scholars Press, 1984. Chinese translation, 2002. Reprinted by Global Scholarly Publications, New York, 2006.

Chinese Texts and Philosophical Contexts: Essays Dedicated to Angus C. Graham. La Salle, IL: Open Court, 1991.

Metaphilosophy and Chinese Thought. With Ewing Chinn. New York: Global Scholarly Publications, 2005.

Books Translated and Edited

Discourse on the Natural Theology of the Chinese by Gottfried W. Leibniz. With Daniel J. Cook. Society for Asian and Comparative Philosophy Monograph Series, no. 4. Honolulu: University of Hawai'i Press, 1977. 2nd printing, 1980.

Leibniz: Writings on China. With Daniel J. Cook. La Salle, IL: Open Court, 1994. Chinese translation 2006.

The Analects of Confucius. With Roger T. Ames. New York: Ballantine, 1998. Chinese translation, 2003.

The Classic of Family Reverence: A Philosophical Translation of the Xiao Jing. With Roger T. Ames. Honolulu: University of Hawai'i Press, 2008.

THE INSTITUTE
FOR WORLD RELIGIONS

The Institute for World Religions was established as a direct result of the inspiration and planning of the Venerable Master Hsüan Hua and Paul Cardinal Yü Bin. Both of these distinguished international leaders in religion and education believed that harmony among the world's religions is an indispensable prerequisite for a just and peaceful world. Both shared the conviction that every religion should affirm humanity's common bonds and rise above narrow sectarian differences.

When they established the Institute for World Religions in 1976, Cardinal Yü Bin enthusiastically agreed to serve as the Institute's first director. In 1994 the Institute moved to the Berkeley Buddhist Monastery. Its proximity to the University of California at Berkeley, Stanford University, the Graduate Theological Union, and to the rich academic, religious, and cultural environment of the San Francisco Bay Area provides an ideal environment for the Institute's programs.

In keeping with its mission, the Institute offers programs designed to bring the major religious traditions together in discourse with each other and with the contemporary world. The Institute also participates in local and global interfaith initiatives as a way to bring the principles of interfaith vision and the spiritual needs of the modern world into constructive engagement.

Among the Institute's programs is the annual Venerable Master Hsüan Hua Memorial Lecture Series, now in its seventh year. The lectures series invites speakers who are grounded in one or another of the great spiritual traditions, and who are immersed in the scholarly investigation of their own tradition and/or the traditions of others. The lectures are subsequently published in the Institute's annual journal, *Religion East & West,* and then expanded into book form and published by Open Court Publishing Company, Chicago.

A BRIEF PORTRAIT
OF THE VENERABLE MASTER
HSÜAN HUA

*T*he Venerable Master Hsüan Hua (1918–1995) was born
into a peasant family in a small village on the Manchurian
plain. He attended school for only two years, during which
he studied the Chinese classics and committed much of
them to memory. As a young teenager, he opened a free
school for both children and adults. He also began one of
his lifelong spiritual practices: reverential bowing. Outdoors,
in all weather, he would make over eight hundred prostrations
daily as a profound gesture of his respect for all that is good
and sacred in the universe.

He was nineteen when his mother died, and for three
years he honored her memory by sitting in meditation in a
hut beside her grave. It was during this time that he made a
resolve to go to America to teach the principles of wisdom.
As a first step, at the end of the period of mourning, he
entered San Yuan Monastery, took as his teacher Master
Chang Zhi, and subsequently received the full ordination
of a Buddhist monk at Pu To Mountain. For ten years he
devoted himself to study of the Buddhist scriptural tradition
and to mastery of both the Esoteric and the Chan schools of
Chinese Buddhism. He had also read and contemplated the
scriptures of Christianity, Daoism, and Islam. Thus, by the
age of thirty, he had already established through his own
experience the four major imperatives of his later ministry in
America: the primacy of the monastic tradition; the essential

role of moral education; the need for Buddhists to ground themselves in traditional spiritual practice and authentic scripture; and, just as essential, the importance and the power of ecumenical respect and understanding.

In 1948, Master Hua traveled south to meet the Venerable Hsü Yun, who was then already 108 years old and China's most distinguished spiritual teacher. From him Master Hua received the patriarchal transmission in the Wei Yang lineage of the Chan school. Master Hua subsequently left China for Hong Kong. He spent a dozen years there, first in seclusion, then later as a teacher at three monasteries which he founded.

Finally, in 1962, he went to the United States, and by 1968, he had established the Buddhist Lecture Hall in a loft in San Francisco's Chinatown. There he began giving nightly lectures in Chinese to an audience of young Americans. His texts were the major scriptures of the Mahayana. In 1969, he astonished the monastic community of Taiwan by sending there for final ordination two American women and three American men, all five fully trained as novices, conversant with Buddhist scripture, and fluent in Chinese. During subsequent years, the Master trained and oversaw the ordination of hundreds of monks and nuns who came to California from every part of the world to study with him. These monastic disciples now teach in the twenty-eight temples, monasteries, and convents that the Master founded in the United States, Canada, and several Asian countries. They are also active, together with many volunteers from the laity, in the work of the Buddhist Text Translation Society, which to date has issued over 130 volumes of translation of the major Mahayana sutras and instructions in practice given by the Master.

As an educator, Master Hua was tireless. From 1968 to the mid-1980s he gave as many as a dozen lectures a week, and he traveled extensively on speaking tours. At the City of Ten Thousand Buddhas in Talmage, California, he established formal training programs for monastics and for laity; elementary and secondary schools for boys and girls; and Dharma Realm Buddhist University, together with its branch, the Institute for World Religions, in Berkeley. In forming the vision for all of these institutions, the Master stressed that moral education must be the foundation for academic learning, just as moral practice must be the basis for spiritual growth.

The Venerable Master insisted on ecumenical respect, and he delighted in interfaith dialogue. He stressed commonalities in religious traditions—above all their emphasis on proper conduct, compassion, and wisdom. He was also a pioneer in building bridges between different Buddhist national traditions. He often brought monks from Theravada countries to California to share the duties of transmitting the precepts of ordination. He invited Catholic priests to celebrate the Mass in the Buddha Hall at the City of Ten Thousand Buddhas, and he developed a late-in-life friendship with Paul Cardinal Yü Bin, the exiled leader of the Catholic Church in China and Taiwan. He once told the cardinal: "You can be a Buddhist among the Catholics, and I'll be a Catholic among Buddhists." To the Master, the essential teachings of all religions could be summed up in a single word: wisdom.

GLOSSARY FOR DIAGRAM

BUDDHIST TERMS

Śūnyatā. Emptiness as essence of all things.

Nirvāṇa. State of perfect tranquility.

Dharmakāya. One of the bodies of the Buddha.

Bodhisattvas. Those who have awakened to the aspiration of enlightenment.

Saṃbogakāya. The "enjoyment body" considered to be the reward of Buddhahood.

apsaras/Devakanyā. Goddesses in general; female devas; attendants on the regents of the sun and moon; wives of Ghandharvas; the division of sexes throughout the devalokas.

Nirmānakāya. The manifest, or body that transforms. The appearance of the Buddha that takes the form of those whom he teaches.

Buddha-Nature (Buddha Gotra). The capacity of all sentient beings to attain to Buddhahood; gotra means "source."

alaya-vijñāna. Storehouse of consciousness, the eighth consciousness, or sensory perception.

mano-vijñāna. The seventh consciousness, the consciousness of the mind, the mind realm—a subtler type of mental functioning.

Saḍ Vijñāna. The six senses, or the sensory perceptions.

HINDU TERMS

Nirguṇa Brahman. *Guṇas* are the three composites of nature. *Nir-guṇas* is nature without the three composites:

> *sattva.* The first of the three composites; the luminous aspect of nature, pure and pacified light that dominates over the being that has attained Knowledge.
>
> *rajas.* That which represents activity and produces movement.
>
> *tamas.* The twilight that dominates animal nature, it connotes ignorance and inertia.

Saguṇa Brahman. *Sa-guṇas* is nature with the three composites. *Brahman* is the most used term for the Absolute in the Hindu tradition. It denotes pure being, pure conscience, the limitless.

Devas in Lokas. *Loka*, world, is the region of the universe distinguished by those who live in, or rule over it.

Prakṛti. Nature; materiality.

Turiya (Ātman). *Ātman* is the personal pronoun that denotes the reflexive of the third person singular: himself. It also denotes the eternal principle that animates the empirical individual. It is the eternal principle which is inside each the human being and asks one to give up all that is material, in order to harmonize with Brahman. It is "human," since only human beings have the possibility of deliverance.

causal body (Jīva). In the *Katha Upanishad* "The individual soul . . . the jīva is one with the universal" (II.1.5).

subtle body (Manas). The mind, subtle body, both an internal organ and the "common sense" that assures the relation between Ātman with all that is empirical.

gross body (Rūpa). The physical body, or the four elements (earth, air, fire, water).

ISLAMIC TERMS

Huwīya Ghaiba. The unmanifested suchness. The term is often translated as He-ness, it-ness, or quiddity.

'Izzah. The inaccessibility of God due to his sovereign power, the strength of possibilities due to the fact that they have no opposites.

al-Jabbarut. The sphere of domination, invincibility, or imaginal world.

al-Malakut. World of dominion, or spiritual world.

al-Mulk. The kingdom of God, or corporeal world.

Note: The standard texts following three terms denote the basic worlds of *both* the macrocosm (universe) *and* the microcosm (human, individual). Some Sufis reverse the order of the last two: **al-mulk**—the kingdom, or corporeal world; **al-jabbarut**—the invincibility, or imaginal world; **al-malakut**—world of dominion, spiritual world).

qalb. The heart as a place of transformation, change, variableness, inconsistency.
The heart is His Throne and not delimited by any specific attribute, it brings together all the divine names and attributes (Qur'an 17:110).

fitrah. The primordial nature of every human being.

rūḥ. Soul.

nafs. Psyche.

jinn. Beings of fire.

Note: According to Ibn 'Arabi and his teachings, the microcosm reflects the macrocosm in two ways: as a hierarchy of existence and as a divine form, a theomorphic entity. Three subsets of the macrocosm are represented in man as: **rūḥ**, the spiritual; **nafs**, imaginal; **jinn**, corporeal. The human spirit is also God's spirit, *al rūḥ al iḍāfī*, i.e., attributed to God. It is a term which suggests its ambiguous status: both divine and human at once.

CHINESE TERMS

Unspeakable Tao 道. The Way; underlying order of things which cannot be named.

T'ien 天. Heaven; what is given by Nature.

shen/kuei. Heaven and Earth.

shen 神. Spirits, the gods, deities; supernatural beings.

kuei 鬼. Ghosts; disembodied spirits.

10,000 Things. The myriad phenomena; "all things under heaven."

shen-t'i 身. Physical body; material human body.

ling 靈. Soul; soul of the departed; spiritual world.

hsin/xin 心. Mind; the heart (as repository of feelings, intelligence, and thought).

INDEX